PLAYING

A

LARGER GAME

PLAYING
A
LARGER GAME

INCARNATING THE POWER OF
EVOLUTIONARY LOVE

BECOMING POWER HUNGRY FOR
THE SAKE OF THE WHOLE

. . .

From Conscious Evolution 1.0 to
Conscious Evolution 2.0

One Mountain, Many Paths: Oral Essays
Volume Twelve

DR. MARC GAFNI and
BARBARA MARX HUBBARD

Author: Marc Gafni and Barbara Marx Hubbard
Title: Playing a Larger Game
From Conscious Evolution 1.0 to Conscious Evolution 2.0

Identifiers: ISBN 979-8-88834-084-4 (electronic)
ISBN 979-8–88834–083–7 (paperback)

Edited by Timothy Paul Aryeh, Dorothea Betz, David Cicerchi, and Terry Nelson

World Philosophy and Religion Press, St. Johnsbury, VT
in conjunction with

IP Integral Publishers

https://worldphilosophyandreligion.org

JOIN THE REVOLUTION!

CONTENTS

EDITORIAL NOTE ABOUT AUTHORSHIP, EDITING, AND THE RADICAL CONTEXT FOR THIS SERIES

ORAL ESSAYS FROM THE ONE MOUNTAIN, MANY PATHS WEEKLY BROADCAST

This volume is part of the Oral Essays library, a series of lightly edited, compiled transcripts of oral teachings given by Dr. Marc Gafni and the late Barbara Marx Hubbard in their weekly online broadcast, *One Mountain, Many Paths,* which they co-founded in 2017. Originally called an "Evolutionary Church," *One Mountain, Many Paths* became a key venue for the articulation of an inspired and deeply grounded new Story of Value in response to the meta-crisis. Marc and Barbara—together with Zak Stein,[1] Kristina Kincaid, Ken Wilber, Sally Kempton, Lori Galperin, Aubrey Marcus and dozens of other thought-leaders over the years—began to articulate what they call a World Philosophy and World Religion[2] as a context for our diversity.

---

1 Zak, together with Ken Wilber, has been Marc's primary intellectual partner and an initiate lineage holder in CosmoErotic Humanism.

2 This project is grounded in four core organizational frameworks: 1) The Center for World Philosophy and Religion, co-founded by Marc Gafni, Zachary Stein, Sally Kempton, and Ken Wilber, and chaired over the years by John P. Mackey, Barbara Marx Hubbard, Aubrey Marcus, Gabrielle Anwar and Shareef Malnik, Carrie Kish and Adam Bellow, and Kathleen J. Brownback. 2) The Office for the Future, chaired by Stephanie Valcke and Ivan Bossyut. 3) The World Philosophy and Religion Press, founded and chaired by Aubrey Marcus, together with Marc Gafni and Zachary Stein. 4) The Foundation for Conscious Evolution, founded by Barbara Marx Hubbard and currently chaired by Peter Fiekowsky. For a complete list of key leadership, see the Office for the Future website, www.officeforthefuture.com.

Until Barbara's passing in 2019, she and Marc transmitted teachings together as evolutionary partners and "whole mates," weaving together insights and transmissions from their decades of practice, study, teaching, and activism into a synergy of wisdom, a grounded vision for future policy across all sectors of society.

Much of the *Dharma* material below comes directly from Marc, so it was originally all in quotation marks—but that looked a little odd. So per his suggestion we removed them, and the reader should consider the paragraphs on the next several pages as one extended quote from him. We are joyfully grateful to Marc for the clarity of his *Dharma*, the elegance and "second simplicity" of this language, and the mad, Outrageous Love with which he transmits his teachings.

Barbara and Marc called the mission of *One Mountain* "a Planetary Awakening in Evolutionary Love Through Unique Self Symphonies." We are an evolutionary community with a deeply grounded, radically alive, and "post-tragic" revolutionary spirit. We are activating a new humanity and awakening as a new species: *Homo amor*, the fulfillment of *Homo sapiens*.

One Mountain is committed to articulating a Story of Value that can become the ground for the new society that must be birthed in response to the meta-crisis. We recognize that we are living at a pivotal moment in history. In this "time between stories," the great moral imperative is to tell the new Story of Value. It is ours to do, personally and collectively, with great trembling and ecstatic joy.

FROM DOGMA TO *DHARMA*: ETERNAL AND EVOLVING FIRST PRINCIPLES AND FIRST VALUES

The teachings are grounded in decades of deep study across many wisdom traditions. Over the years, week by week, these teachings were incrementally developed within the framework of the *One Mountain, Many Paths* broadcast. We often refer to these teachings as *Dharma*.

This word was originally used in lineage traditions to refer to something like universal law. This is a crucial realization: just as there is universal law in mathematical value, there is also a sense of universal law in ethics and value.

Historically, *Dharma* often devolved into unchanging dogma. Evolution was ignored, and the natural process of *Dharma* evolution became disconnected from its deep, eternal context. The weakness of the word *Dharma* is that too often it did not include the evolving insights of the sciences, it confused local cultural truths with universal truths, and it used words like "eternal," as in "eternal Tao," as opposed to words like "evolution."

Eternal came to mean unchanging, and that kind of thinking often led to overly ethnocentric readings of *Dharma*. Local systems would claim their religious and cultural insights as immutable, which stood in the way of the emergence of a genuine world Story of Value that is real, inherent to Cosmos, and backed by the Universe—even as it is also always evolving.

Or, as we often say, "eternal value is evolving value. The eternal Tao is the evolving Tao."

We have shown that, emergent from profound insights in the "interior sciences," eternal does not mean unchanging in time; it means what we call the deeper Field of ErosValue that is beneath culture, geography, and history, which lives beneath all individual and collective values, and beneath time and space itself.

As such, we have gradually transitioned from the term *Dharma* to the term *Value*, in the sense of the Field of Value that lives beneath all values. This Field of Value discloses as First Principles and First Values embedded in a Story of Value.

Indeed, as the interior sciences knew and the exterior sciences imply, Reality arises in a Field of ErosValue in which an entire set of mathematical, musical, molecular, moral, and mystical values are the very ground of all being. That Field of Value is eternal—the true ground of the Good, True and Beautiful—even as it is evolving.

But of course, it is equally critical not just to talk about evolving value, but to ground the evolving value in its true nature, the eternal Field of First Principles and First Values, always reaching for ever-more life, ever-more love, ever-more care, ever-more depth, ever-more uniqueness, ever-more intimate communion, and ever-more transformation.

As such, when we refer to the word *Dharma*, which still appears in these texts together with the word value, we refer to an evolving *Dharma* grounded in an *eternal and evolving* Field of Value. Indeed, eternity and evolution are two faces of the whole, opposites joined at the hip, that characterize the nature of our Cosmos in virtually all of its expressions.

It's in these terms that we ground a robust world philosophy that integrates the validated, leading-edge insights of premodern traditional wisdom, modern wisdom, and more recent postmodern insights, weaving them together into a new whole greater than the sum of its parts.

This new whole is a shared Story of Value rooted in First Principles and First Values that are both eternal and evolving.

These First Principles and First Values of Cosmos are woven together into a new Story of Value as a context for our diversity, a new Universe Story. This new Story gives us the best possible responses we have to the mystery, and to the great questions:

- ◆ Who am I? Who are we?
- ◆ Where am I? Where are we?
- ◆ What should I do? What should we do?

It is only through such a shared Universe Story—a narrative of identity and ethos as a context for our blessed diversity—that we can realize how what unites is so much greater than what divides us.

Only a new Story of Value will allow us to both respond to the meta-crisis and participate together in birthing the most true, good, and beautiful world that we already know is possible.

THIS ORAL ESSAYS SERIES IS AN ENTRYWAY TO THE GREAT LIBRARY OF COSMOEROTIC HUMANISM

This Oral Essays series is part of the overarching project of the Great Library at the Center for World Philosophy and Religion, led by Dr. Marc Gafni, together with Dr. Zak Stein. The aim of the Great Library project is to articulate a robust and comprehensive new Story of Value, CosmoErotic Humanism, in the form of dozens of well-researched and extensively footnoted academic works.

Our vision is to provide the philosophical framework that will be vital for navigating humanity through this time of immense crisis and transformation.

To begin your journey into CosmoErotic Humanism, we tenderly refer you to the book *First Principles and First Values*, co-authored by Marc Gafni, Zak Stein, and Ken Wilber, under the name David J. Temple. David J. Temple is a pseudonym created for enabling ongoing collaborative authorship at the Center for World Philosophy and Religion. The two primary authors behind David J. Temple are Marc Gafni and Zak Stein, and for different projects, specific writers will be named as part of the collaboration, such as Ken Wilber and others.

Three other volumes complete this introduction: *A Return to Eros*, by Marc Gafni and Kristina Kincaid; *Your Unique Self*, by Marc Gafni; and *Education in a Time between Worlds*, by Zak Stein.

We hope that the Oral Essays in this volume, with their informal style of transmission, will serve as an allurement and entryway for you into the more formal books of the Great Library that provide the robust intellectual underpinnings of the new Story of Value.

A NOTE ABOUT THE EDITORS

This Oral Essays collection has been edited by students of the new Story of CosmoErotic Humanism. Each of us has actively participated in *One Mountain, Many Paths*, and most of us have been in deep "Holy of Holies" study with Dr. Marc Gafni for many years.

We have been privileged to find ourselves well-versed in the teachings, and even emerging as lineage-holders of CosmoErotic Humanism.[3]

We view this editing project as a privilege and a deep practice of study and clarification. We experience ourselves as a *mystical editing society*, frequently meeting and conversing together about the content—the depth of knowledge and wisdom offered here—as well as the technical intricacies involved with publishing a beautiful and coherent series of books. In so doing, we function as a "Unique Self Symphony," which itself is a Dharmic

---

3   CosmoErotic Humanism is a world philosophical movement aimed at reconstructing the collapse of value at the core of global culture. Much like Romanticism or Existentialism, CosmoErotic Humanism is not merely a theory but a movement that changes the very mood of Reality. It is an invitation to participate in evolving the source code of consciousness and culture towards a cosmocentric *ethos* for a planetary civilization.

The term CosmoErotic Humanism, initially coined by Dr. Gafni and colleagues, points to a complex, multi-faceted, layered, and nuanced evolutionary set of insights that has evolved over decades of intensive research, teaching, and spiritual practice from deep within a wide range of wisdom traditions (including the Wisdom of Solomon lineage tradition, Bodhisattva Buddhism, and Kashmir Shaivism), as well as multiple disciplines including complexity theory, chaos theory, emergence theory, molecular biology, and the more classical disciplines of the humanities.

The seeds of CosmoErotic Humanism were planted with Dr. Marc Gafni's work on a two-volume, 1,000-page opus called *Radical Kabbalah* (Integral Publishers, 2012). This scholarly work, sourced from deep study within the esoteric lineage texts of the Wisdom of Solomon, points to a non-dual, or acosmic, realization which—unlike the prevailing conceptualization of non-duality—does not efface the human being; rather, it is highly humanistic in its nature. The next step in the evolution of CosmoErotic Humanism was the insight that all of Reality is evolving Eros, which lives in, as, and through the human being.

A failure of Eros leads inexorably to the creation of narratives of "pseudo-eros." CosmoErotic Humanism is a response to the modern mental and social breakdown sourced in the proliferation of multiple forms of pseudo-eros and its broken narratives, such as rivalrous conflict governed by win/lose metrics and the dogmatic denial of intrinsic value in Cosmos, which together generate our current "global intimacy disorder."

term that connotes an omni-considerate collaboration between realized Unique Selves synergizing our unique gifts into a new emergence greater than the sum of the parts. Even as we worked diligently to standardize our editing styles, meeting on a weekly basis to debate the nuances of phrasing, we also operated from within a deep appreciation of the unique style that each editor brought to his or her work. As such, the reader might notice some variation in editing style among the books.

Please note that Dr. Marc Gafni has not reviewed these edited Oral Essays, as he is deeply engaged in writing the formal books of the Great Library. But he has been generous in responding to questions and providing overall guidance in the project. Overall, as Marc's students and students of the *Dharma*, we have made it a key project at the Center to publish these pieces of work relatively independently.

OUR UNIQUE ORAL-ESSAY EDITING STYLE PRESERVES THE ENERGY OF THE ORIGINAL TRANSMISSION

Dr. Marc Gafni is a uniquely gifted teacher whose oral transmission is imbued with a quality that has proven transformative for his students. Many of us feel mystically transformed by both the content and the underlying energy of the transmission style. Therefore, as we like to say, *trust the magic ways the Dharma comes through your unique understanding!*

As Marc's empowered students, colleagues, and beloved friends, we have a deep knowing that these teachings are vital for the survival and thriving of humanity as we know it, and we recognize the importance of publishing his teachings in a written format that will be accessible by future generations. At the same time, we sought to preserve the Eros of the original oral transmission with all of its nuance, power, and depth. Our intention in the editing process, to the greatest extent possible, has been to keep these spoken artifacts intact in order to maintain the flow of the original transmission. We have therefore chosen not to engage in intensive formal editing, as we found that doing so resulted in the loss of the energetic transmission that is so key to fully receiving the *Dharma*.

After experimenting with many ways to present these texts, we developed a specific way of laying out the text on the page. Marc, in collaboration with Zak Stein and Russian intellectual/artist Elena Maslova-Levin—and ultimately all of the editors, through many conversations—developed a unique, artistic presentation of the text, using bolding, italics, bullet points, and other stylistic features which together serve to accentuate the immediacy of the oral transmission.

As part of this editing style, intended to preserve the integrity of the original transmission, we have refrained from removing the frequent recapitulations of key themes. We found that each recapitulation contributes something vital to the rhythm and music beneath the words, like the beating drum of our hearts. These recapitulations not only review previous material but also add important new emphases, perspectives, and elements of the new Story of Value. We ask for your patience as a reader to trust the rhythm of these texts, and we trust you as a reader to have the depth and steadiness to find your way through.

KEY COMPONENTS: LINK TO THE ORIGINAL BROADCAST, EVOLUTIONARY LOVE CODES AND PRAYER

To supplement the written word, each episode includes a QR code linking to the original broadcast on YouTube, as well as occasional links to featured songs and video clips.

Each episode also centers around an "Evolutionary Love Code," formulated by Marc. These codes are part of the ongoing articulation and distillation of the *Dharma* as it unfolds and emerges, week by week, over the course of many years, through the mystical process we call Outrageous Love or Evolutionary Love.

Another core component of the *One Mountain, Many Paths* episodes is what Marc and Barbara called "Evolutionary Prayer." Prayer is experienced in *One Mountain* not in the old fundamentalist sense of a "cosmic vending-machine god" who is alienated from Cosmos. Marc refers to this as the "god you do not and should not believe in"—and he often adds, "the god you don't believe in does not exist."

GOD IS THE INFINITE INTIMATE

In fact, in the *Dharma* of CosmoErotic Humanism, a new name for God has emerged: the "Infinite Intimate," who appears in first-, second-, and third-person expressions. Marc first shared this name as he heard it whispered in 2023, although earlier intimations and formulations of the name appeared as early as 2010.

In first person, God is infinitely alive and as intimate as our own first-person experience.

In second person, God is the infinitely intimate Personhood of Cosmos that knows our name and holds us—the God about whom we say, *whenever we fall, we fall into Her hands.* This is the God who is our Beloved, Father, Mother, Lover, and Evolutionary Partner.

Finally, in third person, God inheres in all of the First Principles and First Values of Cosmos, and in the laws of science (both interior and exterior) that govern manifest Reality.

Therefore, we have a realization of God as not only the Infinity of Power but also the Infinity of Intimacy.

In *One Mountain, Many Paths*, we are reclaiming prayer at a higher level of consciousness. And we are reclaiming prayer as deep, alive, loving, and intimate conversations with God as the Infinite Intimate who knows our name.

REFLECTING ON THE CO-CREATION BETWEEN DR. MARC GAFNI AND BARBARA MARX HUBBARD

Barbara and Marc met five years before Barbara passed. As Barbara said so often, "before I met Marc, I was sure that I was done." Barbara had taught so beautifully for decades, focusing particularly on a powerful articulation of "conscious evolution."

Indeed, it would not be inaccurate to say that Barbara was the greatest storyteller of conscious evolution of her time.

Conscious evolution was also a premise in Marc's thinking, but drawn from an entirely different set of sources and experiences. Barbara drew from the classical sources of evolutionary spirituality, such as Teilhard de Chardin, Buckminster Fuller, and many others. Indeed, she was closely associated with Fuller, and was perhaps de Chardin's most ardent intellectual devotee.

Marc drew a somewhat different vision of conscious evolution from the interior sciences of the great wisdom traditions, with a primary emphasis on what he refers to as the "Solomon lineages," merged together with careful readings of the leading edges of the sciences. In the old version of conscious evolution, the movement from unconscious to conscious was a movement of evolution by chance to evolution by choice.

Together Marc and Barbara evolved the old version of Conscious Evolution, pointing out that evolution itself was always in some sense conscious, but as Marc formulated it, the awakening to conscious evolution refers to the awakening of evolution as human consciousness, coupled with the human realization of being conscious evolution in person, and the human capacity to locate oneself within the context of the larger evolutionary story.

Marc focused his attention on an entirely different dimension of Reality, which he and his colleagues began to call CosmoErotic Humanism. The Intimate Universe, Homo amor, Unique Self and Unique Self Symphonies, God as the Infinity of Intimacy, Eros and the CosmoErotic Universe, distinctions like Role Mate, Soul Mate and Whole Mate, the Four Selves,

Evolutionary Love, Outrageous Love, Evolution: the Love Story of the Universe, First Principles and First Values, Evolving Perennialism, the Evolution of Love, and many more are terms articulated by Gafni and shared with Barbara in their conversation, study, and creative engagement.

Some terms they coined together, for example "a Planetary Awakening in Love through Unique Self Symphonies," where Gafni described Unique Self Symphonies, and Barbara aligned her vision of a planetary Pentecost to Marc's vision of Unique Self Symphonies.

Other key terms were unique and articulated by Barbara, for example: conscious evolution, teleros, telerotic, from joining genes to joining genius, regenopause, vocational arousal, birthing of humanity, synergy engine, and of course her work around what she called the Wheel of Co-creation.

Ultimately, Marc and Barbara attempted to synergize their work in what they called the Wheel of Co-creation 2.0. Barbara and Marc experienced themselves as merging their respective *Dharma* into what they began to refer to as Conscious Evolution 2.0, or later, CosmoErotic Humanism.

The first 129 episodes of One Mountain, Many Paths took place in the last period of Barbara's life and reflect the depth and texture of the stunning evolutionary whole-mate meeting between her and Marc. As Barbara was deep in study with Marc, a lot of what she shared in Evolutionary Church was the *Dharma* of their deep study and collaboration. Although sometimes it may be clear who is speaking, we generally publish these early episodes in what we are calling "one voice." The first 129 episodes, with Marc and Barbara together, have been grouped chronologically. Episodes 130 to 400 and onwards, which were transmitted by Marc, have been grouped by topic.

THE INVITATION

We invite you to find your way into this revolution. Each one of our Unique Selves and unique gifts are desperately needed as we co-create this new

Story of Value together, as part of the covenant between generations, for the sake of the whole.

Let's *play a larger game* and evolve the very source code of consciousness and culture together.

With mad love,

The Editors

LOVE OR DIE

LOCATING OURSELVES: ARTICULATING THE ESSENTIAL CONTEXT FOR THE ONE MOUNTAIN, MANY PATHS ORAL ESSAYS

SETTING OUR INTENTION

Intention setting is everything.

We're here—as da Vinci was with his cohort in the Renaissance—**to play a larger game, to participate in the evolution of love, which is to tell the new Story of Value rooted in First Principles and First Values.**

- Our intention is to recognize the critical historical juncture in which we find ourselves.
- Our intention is to take our seat at the table of history and to say, *we take responsibility for this*.
- Our intention is to participate as revolutionaries for the sake of the whole.

What we're here to do is revolution; revolution for the sake of the evolution of love.

It's a revolution for the sake of the trillions of unborn lives that will not manifest:

- The unborn loves
- The unborn creativity
- The unborn goodness
- The unborn truth
- The unborn beauty

All of it looks to us.

Not because we're engaged in grandiosity. Not at all!

- We're trembling before She.
- We're trembling with joy at the privilege.
- We're trembling with joy at the responsibility.
- We're trembling with joy at the Possibility of Possibility.
- We have to enact a new Story in this moment of time. Because it is only a new Story that can change the vector of history.

The most revolutionary act that we can do—the greatest moral imperative of this time—**is to articulate a new Story at this time between worlds and this time between stories**.

Story is not made up, as postmodernity suggests. **We all live in inescapable frameworks; our framework is the story we live in.** Right now, Reality lives according to win/lose metrics, a story that is generating existential risk. **We need to change that story.**

When we change that story, when we tell a new Story—not a made-up story, but a new Story of Value, rooted in First Principles and First Values—**then it all changes.**

We need to participate in the evolution of the source code of consciousness and culture, which is the evolution of love.

It's the most important, exciting, evolutionary, revolutionary act that we can do to alleviate suffering: to be lovers.

Like Rumi, the great poet of Sufism, we have to be "mad lovers," because it's the only sanity.

To be mad lovers is to see around the corner, to not be so obsessed with the details of the contractions of my life.

Let me see bigger.

Let me take complete care of myself in every possible way, let me completely attend to those in my circle of intimacy and influence, and then—*let me expand my circle.*

That's what we're here for.

- Our intention is to participate in the *LoveForce*, the *LoveIntelligence*, the *LoveBeauty*, the *LoveDesire* that literally animates Cosmos all the way up and all the way down.
- Our intention is to participate in the evolution of love.

[*In the next few pages we will cover some key concepts which are essential to locating ourselves and setting the context for all the One Mountain, Many Paths Oral Essays. —Eds.*]

OVERVIEW: EROS IS NO LONGER A LUXURY—IT'S LOVE OR DIE

Eros is life.

The failure of Eros destroys life.

Our lack of Eros is poised to destroy the world.

All civilizations have fallen because the stories that they lived in were, in some sense, stories based on rivalrous conflict governed by win/lose metrics. Every civilization was weakened by interior polarization caused by the lack of a shared Story of Value.

We now have a global civilization, but we haven't created a shared Story of Value.

We haven't solved the generator functions that caused all civilizations to fall. Our global civilization has exponential technologies and extraction models depleting the Earth of resources that took billions of years to create, which is going to lead to a civilizational collapse.

Existential risk is risk to our very existence.

The choice is clear: love or die.

It's that simple.

Eros is no longer a luxury. It is an absolute necessity for the survival of the individual and the planet.

In the last half a century, modern psychology has documented an age-old truth: a fully nourished baby who is not held in loving arms will die.

So too, our world, both personal and global—even with all the resources of intelligence and technology at our disposal—will die without being held in love, in the embrace of Eros.

We must embrace a personal path of love and a global politics of love.

Not ordinary love. Not love which is "mere human sentiment," but Eros, or what we sometimes call Outrageous Love, which is the heart of existence itself.

We live in a world of outrageous pain.

The only response is Outrageous Love.

WHAT IS EROS?

Eros is the experience of radical aliveness, moving towards, seeking, desiring ever-deeper contact and ever-greater wholeness.[4] Eros is the core fabric of Reality's being and the motivational architecture of Reality's becoming.

Eros is what animates the evolutionary impulse itself, from the very inception of Cosmos all the way to our very selves, who awaken to the realization that the evolutionary impulse throbs uniquely in each of us.

The realization of human awakening and transformation that lies at the core of the interior sciences is the invitation—or even the urgent and desperate demand—of a madly loving Cosmos animated by infinities of power and infinities of intimacy.

The demand—the desperate invitation, the plea, the tender and fierce command of Cosmos that lives inside every human being—is to awaken: to awaken to our true nature as unique incarnations of Eros and Ethos that are needed and desperately desired by All-That-Is. Said slightly differently: Reality is Eros. Or: God is Eros.

The failure of Eros destroys life. The collapse of Eros is always the hidden (or not so hidden) root cause for the collapse of ethics.

---

4 We define Eros through what we refer to as the Eros equation (one of a series of what we call interior science equations):

> Eros = Radical Aliveness x Desiring (Growing + Seeking) x Deeper Contact x Greater Wholeness x Self Actualization/Self Transcendence (Creation [Destruction])

There are good reasons for the formal language of the interior science equations in these writings, and the reader is invited to explore them on their own, in particular, in our work, David J. Temple, *First Principles and First Values: Forty-Two Propositions on CosmoErotic Humanism, the Meta-Crisis, and the World to Come* (World Philosophy and Religion, 2024).

This is true both personally and collectively. We live in a moment of a worldwide and personal collapse of Eros. Our lack of Eros is poised to destroy the world. Humanity is currently experiencing what has come to be known as existential risk, a risk to our very existence, or what I will refer to as the Second Shock of Existence.

EXISTENTIAL RISK: THE SECOND SHOCK OF EXISTENCE

The first shock of existence is the death of the human being—the realization that we will die, which dawns in human consciousness at the beginning of history. We are not talking about the biological fact of death but the *existential* realization of death. Although the interior sciences disclose that death is a portal between two days (there is vast empirical,[5] philosophical,[6] and anthro-ontological evidence[7] for the continuity of consciousness[8]), death is also, in our own direct surface experience, a stark end. And that is obviously not a bug, but a feature in the system.

---

5   We refer to evidence gathered by the most serious of researchers, beginning with Henry and Edith Sedgwick at Cambridge University and William James at Harvard University, and continuing in highly rigorous form for the last 150 years, as recapitulated by Whiteheadian scholar David Ray Griffin in multiple volumes. See also, for example, Dean Radin, *Real Magic: Unlocking Your Natural Psychic Abilities to Create Everyday Miracles* (Potter/TenSpeed/Harmony, 2018), *The Conscious Universe: The Scientific Truth of Psychic Phenomena* (HarperCollins, 2010), and other books. Or see the earlier classic by Frederic William Henry Myers, *Human Personality and Its Survival of Bodily Death* (Longmans, Green, 1907).

6   This requires a cogent analysis of materialism and dualism, and the introduction of the far more cogent third possibility, which we have called "pan-interiority."

7   We discuss Anthro-Ontology in some depth in *First Principles and First Values*, and see also the fuller conversation in David J. Temple, *First Principles and First Values: Towards an Evolving Perennialism: Introducing the Anthro-Ontological Method*—both published by World Philosophy and Religion Press, in conjunction with Integral Publishers. For now, we will simply define it as an "innate and clear interior gnosis directly available to the human being."

8   See Dr. Marc Gafni and Dr. Zachary Stein's essay in preparation, "Beyond Death: Anthro-Ontology, Philosophy, and Empiricism." This essay is slated to appear in the book *Towards a World Religion: Homo amor Essays*. The essay is also the ground for a larger book by the same authors, *Twelve Portals to Life Beyond Death: Responding to the Second Shock of*

Our first-person experience is that death ends this life. It is not the *totality* of our experience if we go deeper inside, but it is obviously intended to be the central, potent, and painful dimension of every human life. Indeed, as Ernest Becker potently reminded us, the denial of death is at our peril.

All the stories and all the plotlines and all the threads of living end at that moment. Whatever happens beyond, we have an actual experience of ending. **Paradoxically, that ending, the experience of the finality of mortality, is what presses us into life.** From the implicit demand of the first shock of existence, human beings were activated and pressed into creative emergence, and what emerged was all of human culture, both interior and exterior.

The second shock of existence is the realization of the potential death of all humanity. After all the stages of human history—matter, life, and mind in all of their stages of evolutionary unfolding—we have come to this place in the evolution of humanity, in which the gap between our exponentially expanding exterior technologies and our stalled (or even regressing) interior technologies of value has created dire catastrophic and existential risks.

This gap generates extraction models and exponential growth curves, rivalrous conflicts based on win/lose metrics, tragedies of the commons, and multipolar traps, in which everyone has to keep producing to the nth degree, including weaponized exponential threats to our very existence because we are afraid that the other parties are going to do it and not be transparent—hide it from us and then dominate us.

GENERATOR FUNCTIONS FOR EXISTENTIAL RISK

Let's outline clearly the main *generator functions for existential risk*.

Existence, in which we discuss three forms of material: the empirical, the philosophical, and the anthro-ontological, and show how each form discredits the notion of death as the end.

Rivalrous conflicts governed by zero-sum, win/lose metrics. Rivalrous conflicts generate extraction models at the core of the economic system and exponential growth curves. Both of these drive and are driven by a contrived system of artificially manufactured desires and needs, delivered into culture by ever more precise forms of micro-targeting to individuals and groups through the ever more immersive environment of the internet.

Next, rivalrous conflicts and exponential growth curves animated by win/lose metrics generate **complicated, fragile world systems** highly vulnerable to myriad forms of collapse. Fragile local systems are made exponentially more fragile on a global level by our inability to meet global challenges with social, legal, political, economic, and ethical infrastructures that remain largely local.

All of this is a direct result of the failure to develop more adequate interior technologies that would be sufficiently compelling to displace "rivalrous conflict governed by win/lose metrics" as the motivational architecture for the human life world.

This failure has led to the conditions that will cause the implosion of systems that are already and quite literally on the brink of collapsing themselves. That's what we mean by the *second shock of existence.*

To recapitulate: the second shock of existence is not the death of the human being, but the potential death of humanity.

It is the *Death Star* moment of our species.

THE DECONSTRUCTION OF INTRINSIC VALUE

We stand in this moment poised between utopia and dystopia, at a time between worlds and a time between stories. We need a new Story of Value, eternal yet evolving, rooted in First Principles and First Values, which would become a universal grammar of value and a context for our diversity.

This is exactly what the Renaissance was. It was a time between worlds and a time between stories. In the Renaissance, we had recently been challenged by the Black Death, a pandemic that swept across Europe. The Black Death destroyed between a third to half of Europe and a huge part of Asia. People died horrifically, brutally, in the streets. They had no idea how to meet this challenge, and so, in response to the Black Death, da Vinci and Ficino and their cohorts understood that they had to tell a new Story of Value.

That story was the story of modernity. Did they get it right?

- They got part of it right, which birthed, to use Jürgen Habermas' phrase, "the dignities of modernity," such as new ways of gathering information and universal human rights.
- But they also deconstructed the source of Value. They lost the basis for the Good, the True, and the Beautiful.

The basis used to be divine revelation: *God told us*. But this claim was owned by religion, and every religion began to overreach and over-claim. The revelation was thus often mediated through cultural categories and wasn't fully accurate.

Modernity threw out revelation, but was unable to establish a new basis for value.

Value was just assumed to be real. As it says in the founding document of the American Revolution: *We hold these truths to be self-evident*—that is, *we don't really have a basis for value; we just take it as a given.*

In other words, modernity took out a loan of social capital from the traditional world. The source of value was never worked out.

And then, gradually, value began to collapse.

- The Universe Story began to collapse.
- The belief that the Good, the True, and the Beautiful are real began to collapse.
- The belief that Love is real began to collapse.

As Bertrand Russell is reported to have said, "I cannot see how to refute the arguments for the subjectivity of ethical values, but I find myself incapable of believing that all that is wrong with wanton cruelty is that I do not like it."

What do you do if you grew up in a world in which value is not real? A world without a source of value, without a Universe Story, without a story of human identity, without a story of desire, without a narrative of power?

In the words of W.B. Yeats, *the center does not hold*.

- You have a collapse at the very center of society, because you no longer have Eros.
- You no longer have a Reality in which value is real, and so you have this lingering sense of emptiness.
- You have a complete collapse at the very center.
- We become *the hollow men and the stuffed men*, gesture without form.

And that's the source of our current existential risk.

THE DEEPER ROOT CAUSE OF THE META-CRISIS: A GLOBAL INTIMACY DISORDER

Above, I have outlined the major generator functions of existential risk. But there is a deeper cause for the existential risk that lurks underneath the rivalrous conflict governed by win/lose metrics and the fragile systems they engender.

And we cannot take the Death Star down without discerning and addressing this. We have already alluded to this root cause above, but at this point we need to make it more explicit so that, from this context, the adequate root response will become clear.

Modernity threw out the revelation, but was unable to establish a new basis for value.

This ostensibly surprising statement can be understood in a few simple steps:

1. All of the catastrophic and existential risk challenges we face are global: from climate change to artificial intelligence, pandemics, systems collapse, and exponential arms races.
2. Every global challenge self-evidently requires a global solution.
3. Global solutions can only be implemented with global co-ordination.
4. Global co-ordination is impossible without global coherence.
5. Global coherence is only possible if there is a global resonance between the parts.
6. Global resonance is only possible if we have global intimacy.

ONLY A SHARED STORY OF VALUE CAN GENERATE GLOBAL INTIMACY

Global intimacy—just like intimacy in a couple—is only possible when there is a shared story.

Not just a shared history, but a shared Story of Value.

*   It is only a shared global story that can generate a new emergent quality of intimacy: global intimacy.
*   A shared Story of Value must be rooted in shared ordinating values, or what we have called evolving First Values and First Principles.
*   Intimacy requires a shared grammar of value as a matrix for

a shared Story of Value.

The global intimacy disorder is the root cause for existential risk. The global intimacy disorder underlies the core generator functions for existential risk.

The global intimacy disorder is rooted in the failure to experience ourselves in a field of shared intrinsic value. This failure derives from the deconstruction of value.

Indeed, it is wholly accurate to say that **the root cause of the two generator functions of existential risk is the failed story of intrinsic value, or what we might also call the breakdown of Eros.**

1. The first generator function is **the success story**. Our modern success story is rivalrous conflict governed by win/lose metrics, which violates all the terms of the Intimacy Equation: there is no shared identity and no mutuality of recognition, feeling, value or purpose, and instead of *relative* otherness, there is *alienated* otherness. Such a story generates complicated fragile systems with no allurement or intimacy between the parts, systems which optimize for efficiency (as an expression of win/lose metrics) and not for resiliency and life.

2. The second generator function is **the deconstruction of intrinsic value** itself. The deconstruction of value is the sense that human value does not participate in the intrinsic value of the Real, for the Real is dogmatically declared to have no intrinsic value. Thus, there is no shared identity between the interior of the human being and Reality. There is no common participation in a field of shared intrinsic value. Instead of being intimate with value, we are alienated from value. And only intrinsic value can arouse will: political, moral, and social will.

To sum up, without a shared grammar of value there is no global intimacy, and therefore no global coherence, and no global coordination in response to catastrophic and existential risk, which means, put simply, there will be, quite literally, no future.

HEALING THE GLOBAL INTIMACY DISORDER REQUIRES THE EVOLUTION OF INTIMACY

But we are not hopeless. On the contrary, we are filled with great hope. Hope is a memory of the future. That memory of the future *is* the direct hit that takes down the Death Star, the culture of death. **The direct hit must be**—as it has always been in history—**the emergence of a new stage of evolution**.

Crisis is an evolutionary driver, and every crisis is, at its core, a crisis of intimacy: from the oxygen crisis of the single cells dying which generated multicellular life at the dawn of existence, to the existential risk in this very moment.[9]

The direct hit is therefore structurally self-evident: the evolution of intimacy itself.

What is intimacy, as a structure of Cosmos all the way down and all the way up the evolutionary chain? We engage this inquiry in depth in other writings, but for now we will simply adduce what we have called the "Intimacy Equation":

---

9 We demonstrate this principle in some depth in the multi-volume series, *The Universe: A Love Story* (forthcoming) (https://worldphilosophyandreligion.org/early-ontologies), *The Intimate Universe: Global Intimacy Disorder as Cause for Global Action Paralysis* (forthcoming), and in other writings of CosmoErotic Humanism.

Intimacy = shared identity in the context of [relative] otherness x mutuality of recognition x mutuality of pathos x mutuality of value x mutuality of purpose

Intimacy is about the capacity of parts to generate a *shared identity* while retaining their otherness, or distinct identity. This requires multiple mutualities, including recognition, pathos (or feeling), value, and purpose. The parts must recognize and feel each other, even as they share value and purpose. But all of this must lead to intimate union—and not pathological fusion, where the distinct identity of the parts disappears—like subatomic particles that successfully become an atom, or two people who successfully become a couple.

THE DECONSTRUCTION OF VALUE IS THE DECONSTRUCTION OF INTIMACY

We have identified the global intimacy disorder as the root cause of existential risk. But the underlying ultimate failure of intimacy is the deconstruction of value itself.

The deconstruction of value means that human value does not participate in any sense of intrinsic value of the Real. This is not about individual *values,* but about *the Field of Value* that underlies all of them. **When the human being**—moved, often sincerely or even nobly, by myriad cultural, historical, and psychological confusions—**claims to have stepped out of the Field of Value, then intimacy itself is deconstructed.**

The deconstruction of value is the deconstruction of intimacy.

In the absence of a shared Story of Value, a story that is an authentic expression of Reality's Eros, a story rooted in *pseudo-Eros* takes center stage and becomes the generator function for existential risk. Our modern pseudo-Eros story is *rivalrous conflict governed by win/lose metrics.* Such a story catalyzes in its wake the second generator function of existential risk: *complicated fragile systems with no allurement or intimacy between the parts*. It is in that sense that we have argued that the first generator function for existential risk is the success story.

- The failure of intimacy is precisely the impotent experience that there is no shared identity between the interior of the human being and Reality. **There is no shared identity in the sense of any kind of common participation in a field of shared intrinsic value.**

- **But only a shared Story of Value can arouse the global will required to engage catastrophic and existential risk.** For it is only global political, moral, and social will—and we can even say *erotic* will—that can generate the most Good, True and Beautiful world that we have always known is possible.

THE EVOLUTION OF LOVE IS THE TELLING OF A NEW STORY

Coupled with the Intimacy Equation is the scientifically grounded realization, in both the exterior and interior sciences, that Reality is a progressive deepening of intimacies, or, said slightly differently:

Reality is Evolution. Evolution is the evolution of intimacy.

- The evolution of intimacy requires—both personally and collectively—a deeper, more accurate discernment of the nature of our Universe, ourselves, and our beloveds.
- This new discernment generates a new global Story of Value.
- The new global Story of Value generates an emergent, heretofore unseen global intimacy and heals the global intimacy disorder.

The new Story of Value is the direct hit that takes down the Death Star and replaces it with the hope that invokes the memory of our best future.

Global intimacy facilitates global coherence, which facilitates global coordination, which activates the possibility of our creative and effectively coordinated global responses to the global meta-crisis in its entirety and its specific expressions.

To solve Bertrand Russell's challenge—the apparent argument for the subjectivity of ethical values—**we have to reground value theory in eternal yet evolving First Principles and First Values, and articulate a new Story of Value**.

This is what we call CosmoErotic Humanism.

CosmoErotic Humanism—together with other emergent strands—**needs to become the ground of a world religion as a context for our diversity**. We need religion, even as we need science, to articulate a shared global grammar of value.

As we said at the beginning, our choice is simple: love or die.

- To love means to participate in the evolution of love, which is the evolution of the human Story of Value.
- To love means to evolve and activate a new cultural enlightenment—rooted in a new narrative of identity, a new narrative of value, a new narrative of intimate communion, a new narrative of desire, a new narrative of power—all of which will birth new narratives of economics and politics.
- The evolution of love is the telling of a new Story.

The new Story that must be told is a love story, for in fact that is the deepest truth of Reality, rooted in the best exterior and interior sciences, that we have at this moment in time:

- Reality is not merely a fact. Reality is a story.
- Reality is not an ordinary story. Reality is a love story.
- Reality is not an ordinary love story. Reality is an Outrageous Love Story.

Story doesn't mean it's *made-up*.

It means doing the hard work of integrating the validated insights of the traditional world, the modern world, and the postmodern world.

This is the intention at the heart of telling the new Story of CosmoErotic Humanism.

ABOUT THIS VOLUME

We live in a time of global crisis. The crisis affects virtually every vector of our lives, from politics to religion to relationships to mental health to systems breakdown to artificial intelligence, and more. All of the crises are interlinked at their core, expressions of what we have called a "global intimacy disorder." The urgent need for coherent action is existential.

But first, we need to understand that every crisis has the potential to be a birth. Crisis is an evolutionary driver.

In this volume, we explore the birthing process. We feel into the fascinating facets of the evolutionary impulse that support the emergent world yearning to be born.

Evolution is not something that happens "out there." Evolution is not happening *to us*. Rather, evolution is happening *in* us. We live in evolution even as evolution lives in us. We are called to radically realize and be lived as the transformation. We are participatory in the transformation.

Our power and greatest pleasure is the capacity for transformation. We begin with our own transformation. But as we deepen into gnosis we realize that our transformation itself ripples out in all of Reality, ultimately transforming the whole thing.

As we've noted, one of the major drivers of the meta-crisis is a global intimacy disorder. To address this, we must deepen our intimacies—both through their intensification and refinement, becoming ever more open, kind, and committed, and by widening our circles of intimacy in our personal lives. In doing so, we directly heal and transform the whole.

We need to widen our circles of intimacy beyond egocentric (ourselves), ethnocentric (family and close colleagues and friends), worldcentric (humanity), to cosmocentric (the entire Universe), where we develop care for and intimacy with all of life.

We become all in for all life. We realize that it is all alive, and that the old split between sentience and non-sentience no longer holds.

The challenge for all of us is to deeply feel both the pain and pleasure of the whole.

There is very rarely birth without pain. Our willingness to unguard our hearts and feel Reality's throbbing pain also gives us access to her throbbing pleasure.

Reality is driven by Eros.

The interior of Eros is pleasure.

The highest pleasure is transformation.

Every human being is born to affect a unique personal and a unique social transformation. To fulfill this call is the greatest pleasure. We need to claim our power of transformation.

When we do so, we are filled with a deep sense of purpose and power. It is only then that we can stop playing superficial power games. We re-write the source code of Reality towards a future that works for everyone.

We are not trivial. We become bored with our knee-jerk humility even as we embrace our vulnerability.

We are willing to encounter our cosmic significance.

We realize that love and power are not opposites.

The love of power is inseparable from the power of love.

We explore three authentic forms of power: *power over, power for, and power of.*

We will show that all three forms of power are sacred if they are born from clarified desire and allurement. We must commit to clarifying our desire, leaning into our unique risk, reaching for our unique allurement, and activating our unique capacity for healing and transformation.

As we participate in the cosmic drive and allurement for pleasure, intimacy, and uniqueness, it is up to us to open to this current within us, which indeed are the very core of our identity. Taking our unique risk becomes the road to both responsibility and rapture. We are able to stand in the trembling joy of responsibility. We show up as Evolutionary Lovers on the abyss of darkness and proclaim, *Let there be Light.*

Volume 12

These oral essays are edited talks delivered by Marc Gafni and Barbara Marx Hubbard between December 2018 and January 2019.

CHAPTER ONE

CRISIS OF INTIMACY AND THE PLEASURE OF TRANSFORMATION

Episode 111 — December 1, 2018

EVOLUTIONARY LOVE CODE: PERSONAL TRANSFORMATION EFFECTS TRANSFORMATION OF THE WHOLE

> Our crisis is a birth, personally and collectively, because our crisis is an evolutionary driver. Every great crisis is, at its root, a crisis of intimacy. Crisis means that someone or something is left out. In every crisis, ask yourself the question, what's being left out of the circle? The solution to the crisis is a new configuration of intimacy.

We each are unique configurations of intimacy. Whatever crisis we may be facing will be healed through a deeper integration of intimacy, starting here, right now, and moving out into the rest of our lives and into the entire suffering Earth.

What we want to do here is to bring together the codes that we were doing for three or four weeks and the new code. There are two sets of codes:

1

One set of codes is about:

Every crisis is a crisis of intimacy.
Crisis is an evolutionary driver.

A crisis of intimacy begs us to ask, *what was left out of the circle*? Intimacy means shared identity. We share identity. We feel each other. When something is left out of *my* identity—some part of myself, some expression of my greatness or shadow—then there is a crisis of intimacy.

When I am only *egocentric* in my love for the group of people around me— my husband, my family, my survival people—when I am not *ethnocentric*, I am not *worldcentric*, I am not *cosmocentric*, then I am leaving people out of the circle. There are different ways that we leave people out of the circle and create a crisis of intimacy. **Whenever anything is left out of the circle, there is a crisis of intimacy.** We restore intimacy by bringing back into the circle that which was left out. That is one set of codes.

The second set of codes, which we will integrate with the first set, is:

Reality is driven by pleasure.

The highest pleasure is transformation. The highest pleasure of transformation is that you can actually transform the whole thing. How do you transform the whole thing? By effecting your unique, personal transformation. We talked before about the question, *what is my personal transformation?*

If you want to know what your personal point of transformation is, which transforms the whole thing, then look in your life at the places where something is left out of the circle, where there is a crisis of intimacy.

In other words, every person has a place where they want to have intimacy, they want to be close, they want to be authentic, they want to be in. We want to be radically alive. We want to have this deep shared identity. It is clearly something that is related to my life, it is part of my life. But now, I can't find intimacy in that place. It could be with myself. I can't find that part of myself that can show up in my full greatness because—I have to look at the *because*.

Usually, it's because I can't open my heart in a particular way, or because I haven't integrated a certain piece of shadow that I am not looking at clearly, which I am avoiding.

Or there is a person I need to get deeper with, and I don't want to because I don't want to give up being right. There are all sorts of things that create our crisis of intimacy.

Or it could be I am just thinking too small. I am just not thinking big enough. I am thinking about my own very narrow tapestry. I am not willing to participate in the evolution of love.

One of the ways I broaden my intimacy is that I'm going to play a larger game, and I'm going to realize that by healing my crisis of intimacy within myself, I participate in the evolution of love.

Here is what it means. Here is where the codes come together:

- Reality is driven by pleasure.
- The highest pleasure is transformation.
- Every human being is born to effect their unique personal transformation.
- Wisdom is knowing what is yours to transform and what is not.
- The highest transformation is the transformation of everything.
- The highest knowing is to know that your radical commitment to your unique transformation is what transforms everything.

And now, add the first set of codes, which is:

- Crisis is an evolutionary driver.
- Every crisis is a crisis of intimacy.

Those two codes speak to each other because if you want to know what your personal point of unique transformation is, you have to identify the place in your life where you want profound intimacy but you can't quite find it. **To recognize that crisis of intimacy in your life, and the healing that comes from crisis, is your personal point of transformation.**

To heal the crisis of intimacy doesn't necessarily mean that you find a partner who's different from your partner, or that you have more long, soulful talks while looking deeply into someone's eyes. Finding a new partner may be necessary at times. Deep, soulful talks are beautiful, but that is not what intimacy means.

Intimacy means shared identity in the context of otherness. Intimacy means that I step out of my narcissism, I step out of my egocentric context. I step into the optimum point of discomfort, and I open my heart in the places where it is hard for me to open my heart. In other words, what it means is that something is left out of my circle of intimacy.

What's left out of my circle of intimacy could be that I can't see my impact on people. How about that?

Or what's left out of my circle of intimacy is that I can't sit in the deep silence, in the goodness of my own being, so I am always trying to cover up the hole of emptiness by moving quickly, impulsively.

Or my emptiness might be that I haven't accessed the realization that I am a good child of the Universe. If I don't know that deep inside myself, I am always moving towards people in a way that wants them to make me good—while coming from *I'm not good*. If I am always waiting for a person to say, *I love you*, instead of me saying, *You love me*, then the realization that I am a good child of the Universe will always be left out of the circle. If you bring it back in, then you realize that it is not, *I love you,* but, *You love me.* I sit in my goodness.

Find your crisis of intimacy and you will find your personal point of transformation. Take that into your prayer.

EXPANDING INTIMACY BY FINDING MY OPTIMUM POINT OF DISCOMFORT

Here is the essence of this week:

- ◆ Are you willing to play a larger game?
- ◆ Are you willing to be an Outrageous Lover?
- ◆ Are you willing to participate in the evolution of love?

Here is the paradox: You participate in the evolution of love by knowing that your love story is personally implicated, that it is chapter and verse in The Universe: A Love Story.

When I find my crisis of intimacy—it could be with my partner that I have been with for twenty-five years—**I can break through to a new level.** It could be with myself. It could be by expanding beyond my narrow circle by stepping out and bringing in someone new, or a new project, or a new gift into my circle. I expand my circle of intimacy.

I stop repeating yesterday. I do that, always, by finding my optimum point of discomfort. What is not comfortable for me? Where is it hard for me? Where is it not default? How do I listen in and feel someone else? That is what intimacy means: we have shared identity, and we feel each other. I feel beyond myself. In that *empathos,* I create a new intimacy, and I transform something inside of me.

So, let's pray to the Divine, who is the Infinity of Intimacy, to evolve our own capacity for intimacy.

It is going to look more different than you think. You think that it is a new boyfriend, it is a new girlfriend, it is a new partner. Or maybe you think it is more time in deep, soulful talks.

No! Intimacy is much deeper than that. Intimacy means I can find that point of discomfort, feel deeply beyond myself, and feel *empathos*—where another person is, or another cause is, or another part of myself is that I have left out of the circle. I bring it into the circle, and I transform something.

I will tell you a holy secret. **Most people in the world never transform.** They just don't. Adult transformation, according to developmental psychology, stops at age 26 at most. Most people keep saying the same thing again and again and again—the same old lines. They just keep saying it again and again, and then they die!

Transformation means I have new lines because there is a new intimacy. There is a new emergence, there is a new revelation and there is something new happening.

- Are you prepared to have this be a new day?
- Can a *new you* emerge?
- Can you find a new intimacy with yourself?
- Can you find your optimum point of discomfort and say, *there is my personal point of transformation*?

When I can do that—when I can be today something new and get *newer every day*—I discover this is actually the truth of evolutionary spirituality. That's an ontological truth. I get newer, but I only get newer if a new me shows up. I don't get newer just because the day passed. **I get newer every day because I disclose a new point of intimacy, a new capacity.**

I stop repeating this old script and I read a new script. I read that new script because I found my personal point of transformation. I found that this is the place where I can become intimate in a new way with myself, with my beloved, with my friends, with my closest people, with my teachers, with my partners, and with my family.

So, are you prepared? Are you prepared to play a larger game? Are we prepared? That means by the end of today! Not later in the day, but by the time you finish reading this. We have to be prepared to find—literally, *for realsies*—a new quality in ourselves.

Can we find a new quality? Find the place that you are so sure that you are right. The place where you have that script, where you keep telling yourself you're right. You know it is this: *You are right, you are right, you are right!*

Give up being right.

Rest in the Goddess and know the goodness of who you are. You don't need to be right to be good. Do you get that? You are so good; we are so good, we are so gorgeous. We can give up being right. You don't have to be right to be good.

Find the place, your optimum point of discomfort, and bring it into prayer.

Where's that place where I can give up being right? The place where I'm already good. I'm wild, a good child of the Universe. I'm held in the arms of the Divine. Every place I fall, I fall into Her hands. I am wildly, gorgeously good, so I don't need to be right.

Find my optimum point of discomfort—*how can I be more?*—and evolution will become more through me: more intimate, more good, more alive, more delighted.

Are you ready? Bring it into prayer. We bring all of it before the Divine, who receives our holy and broken *Hallelujahs*, and say, *Oh my God, you are gorgeous, you are gorgeous. Let me transform with you, today.*

WIDENING OF INTIMACIES AND EMBRACING THE PAIN OF BIRTHING

Radical, radical evolution! I'm looking into myself, asking, *what is that point of transformation?*

I (Barbara) managed, early in my life—let's say when I was in my thirties—to discover evolution. I managed to discover Conscious Evolution and to realize *I am evolution. Everybody is evolution..* Then I fell into an awesome experience of *the intelligence that's in me and in everyone, but also uniquely.* It was really carrying out this very deep thought.

Here was the thing that happened to me, and yet almost nobody around me was feeling this; nobody, particularly the generation I was in, ever thought of this. I felt somewhat excluded and would then try to repeat the story of *evolutionary genius* from the origin of creation. I found myself repeating this over and over because the people around me didn't get it.

My crisis here was that I was lacking new intimacy. And then I met Marc! It was not like I had to try to persuade him about the evolution of life. I didn't have to let Marc know that I believed in the Evolutionary Story of Creation. I met somebody who knew it so well—even more than I knew it—in his particular ways.

Then I lost my old intimacy, the intimacy of being the one who knew something that others didn't know and therefore could share it. I couldn't do that! Since I couldn't do that with Marc, it's our friendship, and our partnership, and our joining genius.

Now, how do you really join genius where somebody already knows 99 percent of what you know but there's like one percent, or maybe a little bit more, that you haven't been intimate with, within yourself—and that can only come out when all the rest of your intimacy is already understood and you don't need to hold it anymore, when you don't need to be its major confessor in the Church of Evolution?

I then began to see the radical newness of the intimacy that comes from this whole *Evolutionary Story*. **I began to feel the depth of sorrow for the hurt that had been given to so many, and out of my joyful nature for having discovered the evolutionary impulse and being sure that it was a great gift of transformation, I** started to experience the sorrow and the suffering of not only us nearby, but the world.

I had a meeting with the leadership of the Urantia Book community. The Urantia Book says our little planet is one of billions of other planets. They have had this information through this channelled work—of the enormity of the Universe and how young we are. There were about twenty people in my living room who were Urantia leaders and they said, *well, we're teaching Conscious Evolution.*

With the people from Urantia, something happened out of the suffering, which was almost blocking my ability to feel the intimacy of evolution. It was very touching in terms of intimacy. They were profound students of what they considered to be the evolution of a universal story so much vaster than Planet Earth, in which there is life everywhere. They seemed to know something about it, as it's written in the Urantia book.

I was able to reconnect with the intimacy of my local version of Conscious Evolution. I was so totally local in comparison to the people from Urantia, and they were helping to encourage me about Planet Earth, as they'd realized it is very early on in its development and there's so much more to come for the planet.

My new intimacy is the willingness to feel all the suffering that there is without trying to make it okay. It's not alright.

There's no way to get around it, and yet our crisis is a birth—and anybody who has had a baby knows this reality. **The suffering that is so profound worldwide, as well as personally in our own lives, is really a crisis of birth.**

The challenge for all of us is to deeply feel the pain as a vital component of what is emerging.

In other words, you do not have birth without pain. It doesn't happen without it.

My point of transformation, and my desire for greater intimacy, is to feel the pain as the intimacy grows, instead of separating pain over here and intimacy over here. I am able to, and it brings tears to my eyes because the depth of the pain is so awesome, and so is the birth!

My revelation and point of transformation is an ability to hold both the pain and the birth, to the extent they happen simultaneously. I had excluded the pain in order to keep in touch with the new story.

YOU CAN FACE THE PAIN WHEN YOU KNOW YOU ARE GOOD

How do you hold this evolutionary optimism and at the same time hold the pain—the enormous pain? That has been our meditation together. Let's reach for this possibility together.

What we are saying is: my point of transformation, my crisis of intimacy, is that in order to hold the joy and the optimism, I have to let the pain in even though I did not want to.

When we let the pain in, all sorts of old stuff comes in. When we let the pain in, the pain of all of us not being held by our mother in the right way comes in and the pain of our father comes in. When we let the pain in, we are afraid that something is going to sneak through the door. **We tried so hard to overcome that old pain with our winning formula in life, and that winning formula has created so much good.**

Am I willing to become more intimate with myself and say, *Oh my God, well I have to let the pain in, and I have to laugh out of one side of my mouth with radical joy and cry out of the other side of my mouth and know that I am held in every second.*

Why are we afraid to let the pain in?

There's something we are not willing to let in because we are afraid that if we let ourselves feel *that*, it is going to be too hard to feel. Actually, it is only when I'm willing to feel *that*, and feel it fully, but not be overwhelmed by it, that I can transform it.

Here's the deep truth: any feeling that I don't feel through to completion remains lingering and then corrupts me. It distorts me. What I have to be willing to do is know that I am strong enough, that I'm held, that I'm madly loved.

I'm not loved just by my mother or father; that may or may not have worked exactly right. But you see, actually:

I am loved by the Infinity of Intimacy that knows my name, that intends me and desires me, chooses me, needs me, adores me and recognizes me.

That is our *dharma*, that is the truth of Cosmos, independent of any individual person. I experience myself *for realsies* as being chosen, recognized, adored, held, desired, and needed. Once I know that deep inside, then I can let all the pain in and let all the joy in. Then the pain and the joy become real together.

Let's try and find a place now where we're willing to be new—willing to let something new in.

- ◆ It might be a pain I wasn't willing to feel.
- ◆ It might be a joy I wasn't willing to own.
- ◆ It might be a dimension of my greatness I wasn't willing to embrace.
- ◆ It might be a kindness that I wasn't willing to live.

Give up the script. Give up the old script. Give up being right. You can give up being right when you know that you're good. We try to be right because we don't think we're good. But when I know that I am good it is really easy to apologize, it is really easy to make a mistake, and it is really easy to change. **I can transform because I don't need to stay with yesterday's script.**

It is for real. *I am new intimacy*. I want to ask you, with total delight, to do something today that shows that you are a new intimacy. Send somebody a note to whom you would never have sent a note before. Send yourself a note. Reach out in a way that you might not have. Soften your voice in a place that might have been hard. Be kind in a place where you might have been *right*.

Don't do it just for yourself; do it for the sake of evolution. You see the difference? It's not a self-help seminar, no!

I am evolution.

Barbara and I (Marc) met when we recognized each other. We recognized that we both lived in the experience. We lived as *I am evolution* because that was our natural truth. We were so relieved. We said, *Oh my God, here is another holy, crazy, beautiful person*, and we were so delighted *for realsies*. I am evolution *for realsies*. I am a new intimacy today.

Now I'm going to reach out and be kind, be soft, or be fierce or give up being right in a way that I would never allow myself to do.

Here is a commitment I (Marc) have always held in life. My commitment is that if I'm wrong, I will apologize. I don't lose my transmission as a teacher. I don't lose the authority of my lineage. I don't lose my dignity. I made a mistake, oh wow! God loves me. I made a mistake. *Sorry, I apologize.* It's so easy!

Do you know why? Because I know I am good. Just give it up. Give up being right because you know you are good and then, be a new intimacy today. It is like, wow! Can you feel that?

Let's go one more step. Just think about it. Perhaps you're going to talk more softly to your partner or feel someone that I haven't felt. Perhaps you will look in the mirror and say, *Oh my God, you are gorgeous!*—and really believe it.

Here are some examples of committing to new intimacies:

- I'll feel more compassion for myself and others.
- I'm going to talk kinder with my sister, while looking in her eyes.
- I'm available and undefended.
- I'm going to send a love note.
- I'm opening and shining forth in a new way.
- I'm going to consciously relax my body and bring down my level of anxiety.
- I'm going to send my mailing list a vulnerable, open newsletter with a new level of openness and vulnerability.
- I'm going to make an authentic apology to my friend.
- I'm going to bring the power of my uprightness.

When I know I'm participating in the evolution of love, I can feel the Goddess writing with me and I feel the breath of eternity and evolution moving through me.

I laugh every day.

I offer one side of my mouth as an Outrageous Lover, and I cry and feel excruciating pain, every day.

When you let your pain and joy become intimate and mix together, something new will be created.

Don't do it just for yourself.

Your self is gorgeous, but do you know why your self is gorgeous? Because you are a *unique expression of the Field of Desire and the field of Love.*

You are—and we all are—needed by All-That-Is.

CHAPTER TWO

THE HOLY TRINITY OF PLEASURE, TRANSFORMATION AND POWER

Episode 112 — December 8, 2018

EVOLUTIONARY LOVE CODE: YOU CAN ONLY TRANSFORM WITH A NEW STORY

As you read this Evolutionary Love Code, think of what it means to you line by line.

> Reality is driven by pleasure. The highest pleasure is transformation. Every human being is born to affect a unique personal transformation. Every human being is born to affect a unique social transformation, more than the *just* personal. Wisdom is knowing what is yours to transform and what is not. The highest transformation is the transformation of everything. The highest knowing is to know that your radical commitment to your unique transformation is what transforms everything.

If I had to characterize the quality of this church, I would characterize it with two qualities. One quality is

Outrageous Love, or Evolutionary Love. There's a sense of Outrageous, Evolutionary Love.

One of our core frameworks is that we live in a world of outrageous pain and the only response to outrageous pain is Outrageous Love. We are a band of Outrageous Lovers disguised as a church, and we are a revolution. We are a wave, a cascading wave of the original Evolutionary Love that initiated and animated the original flaring forth of creation that is now awake and alive in us. It's not ordinary love. It's not a harlequin romance, although a harlequin romance on a good day could be an expression, a spark, of that originating wave of Outrageous or Evolutionary Love.

There is a second quality, and the second quality is what we might call ecstatic urgency. Ecstatic urgency is a particular quality. It is ecstatic, in the sense that it is beyond self. It is *ékstasis* in the original Greek. It is not just *self* in the sense of small self. At the same time, it is not merely the spaciousness of being, gorgeous as that is; but it is urgent. It is the urgency of becoming. We live in a moment in time that's urgent:

- It is difficult to imagine that in the last 23 days in the United States, there was a school shooting virtually every other day. What does that mean? What does that mean that our kids are killing each other?
- When they are not killing each other, they are committing suicide. The rate of teen suicide in the world now is astronomical, and the rate of suicide overall is approaching nearly a million people a year.
- What does it mean that we have nomadic retirees in the United States, for example, who literally can't afford their meals, so they live in their car and go from place to place?
- What does it mean that income inequality is becoming so dramatic that we are living in a world in which people can't take care of their basic needs of human dignity?
- As we move towards the automation of jobs, more and more

16

people in the world are becoming, from the perspective of the elite, extra, useless, not needed.

The evolutionary revolution that needs to take place is a sweeping of Reality with a new set of memetic structures of source codes, of evolved source codes, which emerge from a new Universe Story. If you really want to get the essence of what we believe about transformation, as in the code, it is that **to truly transform, you must transform based on a new Universe Story**. You can't just transform based on feeling good. You have to have an insight—a new insight—into your true identity: what's your new best understanding, based on the best sciences, interior and exterior, of who you are?

What is the new narrative of identity?
What is the new narrative of power?

The answers to those two questions must derive from a new Universe Story. From that place, we have a new narrative of transformation. So, overall, there is a new Universe Story, and within that new story, there is a new narrative of identity and a new narrative of power. We then get to a narrative of transformation. Transformation only happens for real when we have an experience, , literally, of a new narrative of identity: *I realize who I am.*

A NEW NARRATIVE OF POWER—TRANSFORMING THE WORLD BY TRANSFORMING OURSELVES

So, let's go back to the code. Reality is driven by pleasure. The highest pleasure is transformation. Every human is being born to affect a unique personal transformation and a unique social transformation. Wisdom is knowing what is yours to transform and what is not. The highest transformation is the transformation of everything.

Let's add one piece: **The highest pleasure is transformation, and transformation is the highest form of power.**

One of the most important things we need to do is reclaim power as a value. Power is a critical value. I want to invite you to be power hungry. Be power hungry. Desire power. Power is gorgeous.

The highest pleasure is transformation, and transformation is the highest form of power. We are inviting ourselves to desire power—to be power-hungry—because we say in church, *God is not just the Infinity of Power. God is the Infinity of Intimacy.* But God is also the Infinity of Power, and power is unbelievably important.

It is not power over, in the old sense. It is power for.

When I say *power for*, I don't mean it just in that kind of beautiful, New Age-y, liberal sense of power: I am in service.

That is one form of power, and it is beautiful. *Power for* is real, which is distinct from *power over*, which is a dominator hierarchy; rather, *power for*. But power for what? It is not just service.

It is the power of transformation itself. When you think about it: Reality is driven by pleasure. Pleasure is the allurement that drives all Reality, and that brings together, and affects transformation. **What drives the transformation is the evolutionary impulse. The interior quality of the evolutionary impulse is pleasure and power mixed together.** Isn't that awesome? Pleasure and power converge in the evolutionary impulse, and they affect transformation.

What we are trying to do is affect transformation without power, but we can't have the power to transform the world if we don't have the power to transform ourselves.

18

If we don't have the power to transform ourselves, we don't have the power to transform the world. So often, the reason transformation's not working, the reason NGOs aren't working is because we're trying to bypass personal transformation and transform the world. If I don't have the power to transform myself, my unique personal transformation, then I won't have the power to transform the world.

So, my unique personal transformation is based on my power of personal transformation to transform that which is uniquely needing transformation in me.

You can spend all your life doing good works, all your life doing great things, all your life giving great speeches. You can write 20 books, you can write phenomenologies, you can write diaries, you can do whatever you do, but that is what we do naturally. That's just what we do. That's who we are, but there is a point of personal transformation where we must reach.

- We must reach.
- We must shift.
- We must re-pattern.

Evolution's greatness is when evolution *re-patterns*. When we are able to re-pattern, re-patterning is true power. If I can re-pattern, that is my personal transformation.

That personal transformation mystically affects everything. It affects the entire field. It mystically transforms everything. When each of us has that power of transformation, then we come together. That's motivated by Outrageous Love—Outrageous Love of myself and of Reality. Knowing my impact on Reality. Then we can become a band of Outrageous Lovers:

- We don't fall apart based on personal politics.
- We don't fall apart based on non-communication.
- We don't fall apart based on non-intimate divisiveness between us.

Competition and rivalrous conflict within churches, rivalrous conflict within the New Age movement—disguised under all sorts of masks of piety—has prevented us from coming together, because instead of really being committed to transforming the planet, we are really committed to our own labels. We don't really synergize. We don't come together. We don't support each other. We are pretending to be transforming the planet, but really everyone is running a commodification game, and we just happen to be selling transformation, or evolution, or whatever we are selling. That doesn't work.

It's only if we personally transform—and if we're able to give up something precious, to re-pattern our egoic structures, to re-identify as personal, Unique Self-expressions of the evolutionary impulse, to feel that alive in us, to know that my personal unrest is the divine unrest— that we can be whole mates, not just soul mates.

Soul mates are looking for personal fulfillment in each other's eyes. Whole mates are looking at a vision together, joining genius.

What we are trying to model, if anything, is that we can love each other enough to have two teachers come together, and not be branding, but modeling what joining genius in Evolutionary Love means. To model that, it takes heroism, fierceness, and grace.

There are all sorts of voices that are going to tell us, *don't do that, Barbara*, or, *don't do that, Marc*. No one has ever done this before. It is not easy. This is not simple. Joining genius is not simple. It requires enormous love, enormous commitment, enormous integrity, but we want to model an enormous sacrifice. You have to give something up.

So, let's go into prayer, my friends, and let's bring all of the holy and broken *Hallelujahs* that we want to re-pattern. Let's ask God, as the Infinity of Intimacy who is also the Infinity of Power, to give us the divine power of the evolutionary impulse to look at ourselves, to face everything and avoid nothing, and to be fearless—because we know that we are good. We know that we are gorgeous. We know that we are stunning. That is who we are.

We are the goodness of Reality itself, where we are madly in love with ourselves, and when we are madly in love with ourselves, we can give up old patterning. It is okay. We don't need to be right to be good! We can give up being right, and we can claim this new re-patterned vision of ourselves—this new identity—as *Homo amor universalis*. That is what it means to become a new human and a new humanity. That is what it means.

So, let's pray for that. Let's pray for each of us. Pray for yourself and pray for everyone in this community. Pray for everyone that you know. Let's pray to have the power of re-patterning, to literally become the new human. Let's pray that we together can invoke the new humanity.

PERSONAL TRANSFORMATION EFFECTS THE TRANSFORMATION OF THE WHOLE

I want you to be holding, as I do this, the possibility that each one of our prayers is going to give you something of a trajectory that then could go into a convergence of radical power, for you personally, and *beyond you personally*: for the church, and for Eros itself expressed in humanity, because we might as well take it the whole way as we go down into the personal and the local.

The personal leads to the radical transformation of the whole system. You can't get transformed personally without going the whole way, and your *whole way* is a microcosm of the planet's *whole way*. Your personal transformation is a transformation of the whole system, because what it takes for you to truly transform is almost everything inside of you. This occurs in the same way for almost everybody, so we are each enormous personal models for each other.

I (Barbara) don't know anybody this old in the church, and I don't like to call myself an elder, but a *newer*; that is to say, the older you get, the newer you get. Why? Because evolution is always getting new. So, the older you get, the more *newness* you get.

Reality is driven by pleasure. So, get in touch with the deepest pleasure that is driving your reality, and see if you can bring it to your attention, and into a feeling level. What is the pleasure that your reality is driven by, the highest pleasure being transformation? Let's imagine ourselves being transformed by our highest pleasure, and the transformation has to be unique as us. Can you even imagine what going the whole way for you personally might be like? See yourself in that transformation.

Every human being is born to affect a unique personal transformation.

Join me in feeling a transformation that is uniquely personal as you; that is to say, nobody else could have that particular transformation that is you. Dwell on it for a minute, with all the parts of it: *every human being is born to affect a unique personal transformation that is driven by pleasure.*

- ◆ What you begin to see here is the goodness of God.
- ◆ What you begin to see is the goodness of the pattern of creation.
- ◆ What you begin to see here is the divine process of creation, that once you catch hold of it, gives you the incentive to go the whole way yourself, because it is driven by pleasure.

Every human being is born to affect not only a unique personal transformation but a unique social transformation. Think now of how your personal transformation, whatever it is, driven by your deepest pleasure, is affecting a unique social transformation that only you can possibly do.

Think now, and ask yourself: What is your greatest social transformation, that's coming from the pleasure of your unique transformation? What is all the energy in your entire being longing to achieve?

Wisdom is knowing what is yours to transform and what is not. Do you ever try to be transforming what is not yours to transform? Has anybody thought about that? I have. I (Barbara) tried to transform a lot of things that weren't exactly mine to transform—like the political domain, the Democratic Party. Why did I want to run for vice president? I had something in me that wanted to give a speech about the meaning of politics from a platform that was good enough to be heard.

You have to notice if you are doing something what is yours to transform. It might be that what you are doing is your unique social transformation, but it may not be what it objectively looks like. It has to transform you by doing it, and then it transforms the social pattern that you are in, and that is why the vice presidency is a really good example. Everybody now knows—at least anyone who knows anything about anything I have ever done—that **democracy has to evolve**.

When we look at the Wheel of Co-Creation 2.0 that we co-created, it is a pattern that we can put ourselves into, with our deepest heart's desire at the center of the Wheel. In other words, the Wheel 2.0 graphic depicts the patterns of the whole system here, pointing everybody toward knowing how to do it for themselves, and finding exactly where they fit best. To use Jonas Salk's phrase, *it is not survival of the fittest, but survival is what fits best.*

For any one of us to transform the whole way, we have an antenna throughout the system. We couldn't transform the whole way if the system were dying or going to hell, one way or the other.

You may be thinking: *Isn't working on our own transformation selfish?* Working for our own transformation is not selfish, it is a true gift we can give to God.

The pleasure of transformation is the highest form of power.

When you experience this unique transformation that is yours to do, and only yours to do, and you are transformed, your power becomes the power of the system itself through you. You couldn't transform the whole way unless systemically you had connected up to the system.

None of us could go the whole way unless we were systemically part of the living system, and that the living system is affected completely and totally. That is what we are achieving together, folks.

The power of love is the power of the unique transformation of every person going the whole way in this lifetime.

Empowerment of yourself is a power of the universal process of creation embodied uniquely as each one of us. When we say *Yes* to it, the whole system is in each of us, and we are saying yes to our uniqueness.

CLAIM THE PLEASURE OF POWER

We are in the source code of Reality, and we are participating as Outrageous Evolutionary Lovers in evolving the source code itself for the sake of the evolution of love. When kids shoot each other, it means they don't know who they are. It's the despair of not having an identity, of not feeling that I have any power in the world. I go to shoot because I'm grabbing for power. All acting out is a power grab. Do you get that?

---

*All acting out is a form of power grab,
and when we don't have authentic
power, then we go for pseudo-power.*

When we are not hungry for real power, we don't feed ourselves and nourish ourselves with authentic power—which is the unique expression of the evolutionary impulse, alive and awake in me as my Evolutionary Unique Self—then we feed on pseudo-powers, and pseudo-power ultimately is devastating and destructive. Suicide bombers, as I have seen go off in school buses in Israel myself, are grabbing for pseudo-power. People shooting up schools, shooting up in all the ways we shoot up—those are all forms of pseudo-power.

But it is not because we are pathological and depraved. It is because we are healthy, and we are craving real power. **Our culture has deconstructed all forms of authentic noble power and called them social constructions of Reality, and so there is no identity left.** There is no Universe Story, and there is no narrative, and so we feel like we are lost in Kafka's trial, where we are not quite sure where to go, and none of it makes any sense, and so we desperately reach out for some form of aliveness and power.

We are studying the code, and we are awake, and we are alive in the code, and we are loving each other madly and we are intending for the sake of the evolution of love.

Reality is driven by pleasure.

What does that mean? It means that allurement is primary. Why do we gather with friends? Why do we gather in Evolutionary Church? Because we are allured to come together, and allurement is beautiful. We typically hide allurement. We disown allurement. We split off allurement.

Allurement is primary. There is nothing underneath allurement. So, pleasure is allurement, and Reality is driven by allurement through pleasure. We can look at levels of pleasure as:

- Level 1: The pleasure of the five senses in their authentic forms.
- Level 2: The pleasure of love, affection, relationships.
- Level 3: The pleasure of standing for a cause.
- Level 4: The pleasure of true wisdom.
- Level 5: The pleasure of Unique Self creativity, or
- Level 6: The pleasure of the power of transformation itself.

It is all pleasure. The highest pleasure is transformation. Level six pleasure—that is the second sentence in the code. **The highest pleasure is transformation.** Level-six pleasure is the pleasure that I have the power to transform the whole thing. That's the pleasure of knowing that my unrest is the evolutionary unrest. **It's the pleasure of knowing that my yearning participates in the yearning of all being and becoming itself.**

So, the highest pleasure is transformation; but we have now added: *Transformation is the highest form of power.*

We're going to weave this into the source code. We are now together literally weaving, re-weaving the source code of Reality.

THE HOLY TRINITY OF PLEASURE, TRANSFORMATION AND POWER

There is a holy trinity here, and the holy trinity is pleasure, transformation, and power. Pleasure, transformation, and power are a holy trinity that cannot be separated.

Pleasure is driven by power.

Power! Think about the power. Think about it in its shadow side. Think about power, about the addict in the shadow side of pleasure. Pseudo-

26

pleasure moves through everything and overcomes every obstacle to get that fix.

Or think about the power of true love—I am driven by the allurement of true love, and I will turn over the world to get there. I have enormous power, and, Jimi Hendrix, you were awesome on that guitar at Woodstock, you were beyond imagination, but you said that, *the world is going to get better when the power of love is stronger than the love of power.* Jimi, you were awesome on the guitar, but bad at *dharma*. Love and power are not separate:

Love is power, and power is love. Love is filled with power, and we need love to be filled with its power.

So, pleasure is driven by power, and what pleasure and power move toward is transformation—which means quarks come together, and they form a subatomic particle. Subatomic particles±protons, electrons, and neutrons—come together and they form an atom. They are driven by pleasure, by allurement, and they are motivated by the power of evolution itself, which is all of the power in the first nanoseconds of the Big Bang that is running through you and me right now, as we listen, read, talk, and share through the rest.

All that power is the power of the evolutionary impulse, so the highest pleasure is transformation, which is the power of transformation. **When pleasure and power come together, they move us towards creating a new whole, which always happens through transformation. Remember, Eros is radical aliveness seeking ever greater connection and ever greater wholeness.**

When I create a new whole that is me, I am transforming, but it's not a perpetual self-improvement project. No, there's only one project, there is one transformation that is mine to do, and everyone knows what it is. There is a certain point where I have this optimum point of discomfort where I keep falling down in that place.

That is the place where I can turn it around. I never do it all the way, but I spiral up. I then take that same energy and I turn it towards the world, and I engage in transforming the world.

I don't have to wait to transform myself fully, to then transform the world—I can do them together, moving back and forth. We are all imperfect vessels for the light. With my personal transformation, when I really get it—if I can transform myself, if we can see each other, and see ourselves a little more clearly, I transform the world. When we truly transform something in ourselves, give up being right, give up our hidden positions, that personal transformation mystically transforms the whole world.

I want to share a Hebrew phrase to end us with: *Da l'malah, malah mimecha.* The normal way that sentence is translated, from the third century, is: *know that which is above you.* But the evolutionary mystics translate it differently.

They say, *da l'malah*—know that everything that is above—*malah mimecha*—comes from you. That is an ontological statement, it is not psychological. *Da l'malah*—know everything that happens above, **the entire movement, the entire evolutionary pattern of all of Reality,** *malah mimecha*—**comes directly from your personal transformation.**

That is the ontological truth of Reality, that your personal transformation directly in an unmediated form unequivocally ripples through all of cosmos and literally reworks and repatterns and rewires the inner source code of Reality itself.

Let's say I get up and give a big speech in front of 10,000 people, 20,000 people, 50,000 people. I'm giving this great speech, and everyone is blown away, but if I'm on automatic, I've moved almost nothing in the Cosmos. I may be giving a great speech, I'm excited, and of course people are impacted, it's beautiful, and lots of things are moved—but it doesn't have the effect you think it does.

On the other hand, I can be in my room by myself, fighting a sense of inadequacy and depression. I can go in and find the truth—the truth of the fact that I am not separate from all of Reality—and that I am being lived by a larger love, and that every place I have been I needed to be. Then, after finding this place of profound love in myself, I walk outside and get on a bus with a huge smile on my face that came through my personal transformation. I say *hello* to the bus driver, and we have this moment between us. We are both transformed in that moment from a mystical ontological evolutionary perspective that may well transform Reality more than the speech half-heartedly delivered to 50,000 people.

- That is dignity.
- That is power.
- That is real power.

It is knowing that the power lives in us, and *the whole world is a stage*, as Shakespeare said—and he was right. We are always on stage. We are always giving a great speech. The great speeches in history were not the ones that were collected by William Safire in his book 'Great Speeches in American History'.

> *The great speeches in history were given, between lovers late at night and at three in the morning.*

Great speeches were given between friends talking on the phone, between a father and a daughter at a kitchen table, between people taking a walk.

They were given in conversations between us. *I have power, I am power hungry,* and I look at you and I say, *Oh my God, I love you madly.* In that mad love of self and mad love of another, I know that we have power. We are not powerless.

We have to transmit to the kids that are shooting each other, and their entire generation:

You are power!

Power is not abuse; it is not the negative, bad, masculine power. Power is beautiful. Men and women all have power, and that power can reshape Reality.

CHAPTER THREE

TO DENY POWER IS TO DENY GOD: THE THREE FORMS OF POWER

Episode 113 — December 15, 2018

EVOLUTIONARY LOVE CODE: LOVE OF POWER AND POWER OF LOVE ARE INSEPARABLE

Our narrative of power is directly emergent from our narrative of identity, which is directly emergent from our Universe Story, the multi-billion-year story. Power is a divine elixir, nectar and not a poison.

There are three forms of power. The first two forms of power are *power over* and *power for*. Contrary to the popular understanding which deifies *power for* and demonizes *power over,* both forms of power are holy.

The third form of power is the *power of.* All three forms of power are inextricably united, connected with each other—three faces of one.

Love and power are not opposites. The love of power is inseparable from the power of love. The Outrageous Lover is power hungry.

The highest pleasure is the pleasure of power. The highest power is to act and surrender in the same moment: inaction in action, action in inaction.

To deny your full power is to deny God. To deny your full power is to stand against the Good, the True and the Beautiful. Transformation is the highest form of power.

We are delighted and we are powerful!

We want to be power hungry. We are power hungry in Evolutionary Church, but obviously not power hungry in that kind of superficial way where I am extracting from other people their life essence and hijacking it to serve my own egoic superficial insecurity. Obviously, that is not what we mean by power hungry.

If you have noticed, it is a very strange thing that happens in the United States: The Republican Party is not shy about exercising power; they exercise power enormously. Often, the shadows of the Republican Party seem to be exercising power for its own sake. The Democratic Party, who has its own very clear drive for power, is shy about power. It does it behind the scenes, but it always sounds like: *let's talk about noble causes, and power is really not our issue at all.* The Democratic Party disowns power and is all about nobility when actually there is this huge power drive happening all the time. The Republican Party is really focused on power and puts its *nobility* stuff to the side, even though the originating conservative thinking base of the Republican Party had gorgeous noble causes to stand for.

We have this very strange conversation happening about power, and I have to tell you something, the people that I'm most afraid of in the world are people who say, *ah, power, I'm not interested in power.*

People who disown their power drive are dangerous because power gets split off—and then the naked, raw desire for power becomes shadowy and then appears dressed up and under all sorts of noble names.

It appears in the most pathological and terrible ways. So, we need to talk about power. Power is a real thing.

POWER AND INTIMACY ARE INEXTRICABLY LINKED

When we turn to Divinity, to where are we turning?

- ◆ On the one hand, we're not turning away from ourselves because Divinity lives in us, as us, and through us.
- ◆ We're also not turning away from the world because Divinity is the tangible quality, the suchness that animates all of Reality.
- ◆ We are turning to Divinity, as both the suchness quality and creativity of all Reality and that which holds all Reality.

So, God is not a person in the sky, but God is not less personal than a person in the sky. God is not just this abstract other. God is not *the other*. There is a quality of Divinity that is everywhere, and there is a quality of Divinity that holds us and knows us. In Evolutionary Church, we call that the Infinity of Intimacy. It is a phrase from the Unique Self book—the Infinity of Intimacy. God is the Infinity of Intimacy.

When we say God is the Infinity of Intimacy, we mean that God is not only the Infinity of Power; God is also the interior quality of power, which is intimacy. Power and intimacy are not unrelated. Usually, we understand power as being alienated from intimacy.

We're saying, *no, power and intimacy are completely inextricably linked.* We turn to Divinity, who is both the Infinity of Power and the Infinity of Intimacy, who's all of the Good, the True, and the Beautiful—and the most personal gorgeous moments we have ever had—and who holds us in every second.

If we could see all the brainwaves and all the cellular activity and all the atomic activity happening in every one of us and in the space in between us, we would see this dazzlingly allured, inordinately complex, beyond elegant, gorgeous set of the most beautiful interactions—chemical, biological, atomic—happening every second. This is the Infinity of Power and Infinity of Intimacy that knows our name.

What are we saying to God? We are saying, *God, I love you. I love you madly.* Whenever you say I love you, it means I need you. And so, we are saying, I need you, God, I need you so much.

Whenever we say I need you, it means, God, you have power over me, and I surrender. I am powerful enough as an autonomous, powerful human being that I surrender to you, God. I surrender to your power.

But here is the key sentence that takes us into prayer: At the same moment, **God, the Infinite Personhood of Cosmos is saying to us,** *I love you. I love you madly.*

God is saying to us, I need you. I can't do it without you.

We hear God literally turning to us, and saying:

- I love you.
- I need you.
- I can't do it without you.
- You have power over me.
- When I step back to allow room for the world, I was inviting you into partnership.
- I was needing you.
- I need you means you have power over me.

Do you understand? If you are not shivering awake, if you are not exploding out of your heart, mind, and seat, right now, you didn't get that sentence: God is saying, *you have power over me.*

God is saying, I trust you madly and wildly. I am going to surrender my power to you, and I trust you are going to take care of me.

You begin to understand power. There is nothing more joyous than knowing that we all have power over each other, and we trust each other madly to be able to need each other—not in a codependent way. When we say need, we often think *codependent*. We are not codependent.

We are actually, as Fridrich Schleiermacher called it (in German) *Abhängigkeit gefühlt*, the *utter dependency we have on each other.*

We need every single one of us, we need each other. That is what it means to be a band of Outrageous Lovers. With that as our backdrop, we turn to pray. We say to the God who needs us and to the God who we need, Oh my God, I want to bring you everything: my holy and broken *Hallelujah*. Everything. When we pray, we say, *God, help me.* I ask for what I actually need.

TO DENY POWER IS TO DENY GOD

Let's now look at the code: our narrative of power is directly emergent from our narrative of identity, which is directly emergent from our Universe Story. With this, let's open the Universe Story for a moment as a story of love.

If you look at the origin of creation, billions and billions of years ago, and you see the nature of quarks to electrons, to protons, to neutrons, to cells, to multicell, to animals, to humans, and now to us in this church, it is the power of attraction that has created the entire story of evolution.

So, if our narrative of power is directly emergent from the identity that we have with the Universe Story, we might say that our narrative of power is the power of attraction—being attracted by *and* attracting—such that we become intimate with each other by this power of attraction that brought us from quarks to us. So, in the Evolutionary Church, if you can even imagine the thousands of us who have tuned in to be attracted to each other in a new level of intimacy, as in the story of the Universe—do you know what's going to happen?

What's going to happen is an absolutely new humanity and a new culture. That's how it happens. The reason that power is a divine elixir, a nectar, and not a poison, is because we're the power of the Universe expressing uniquely as us.

If we didn't dare express our full power, the Universe could not fully express through us. Think now of your power as a divine elixir. Going in, deeply personal, think of the power to realize all of this potential, it has to be infused with power. Think also of all the things in the Universe that can decline and fail and get lost and get hurt. Think of the power needed to respond to all those things.

That power is God's power in, as, and through you, and it's a beautiful thought—that it's a divine elixir. Feel our power, my power, your power coming from the power of the Universe, which is always creating more.

Through connecting in intimacy, separate parts make a new whole. There is a deep yearning for this church to be a vehicle of our divine power because here we have a field of connectivity that does not necessarily easily exist throughout the entire world. May all of us who are listening or reading this experience that divine elixir. The church is empowering each one of us to do this ourselves, to step into this Divine elixir. We look at our code again:

There are three forms of power. The first form of power is "power over" and the second is "power for." Contrary to the popular understanding, which deifies "power for" and demonizes "power over," both are holy.

Let's say we are deifying our *power for* as the inner impulse of evolution that creates more love, more contact, more creativity, more consciousness, more intelligence. We are deifying our power to express all of that as who we are.

We are also demonizing *power over* when we fall into the illusion of separation and the fear of being more powerful or less powerful than somebody else, and therefore afraid of our own power because we can hurt somebody else. If our power is coming from the God that creates the entire Universe in us, our *power over* is God-like—and we dare not hold it back.

The third form of power is the *power of* which is just as much unexpressed. Here, our narrative of power is for the universal evolution. Our narrative of power, the power of you and me, is the power that creates universal evolution at the personal level and expresses our uniqueness as simply who we truly are. The power of you, the power of me, the power of this whole church, the power of our love of God: that is the *power of* that we are bringing forth.

These three forms of power are inextricably connected to each other—three faces of one.

We are holding it all together—the power of, the power over, the power for—as universal power within us that can create the new human and the new world.

Evolution won't say, *we are going to stop here with just us. This is it folks, we are finished*. No, that is why we must have the *power of* and *power for* and *power over*. Love and power are not opposites. The love of power is inseparable from the power of love. Let's say the love of power is the love of this impulse of creation in the universal story. We *must* be power. We must love it, and to express this power, we are expressing love deeply. This power

PLAYING A LARGER GAME

to express love deeply is making the evolutionary human come alive. I don't think any of us has experienced the full power of the evolutionary human that is being called forth here. **The Outrageous Lover is power hungry.**

As an Outrageous Lover, I want all the power that God can give me to fully express this Evolutionary Love and this evolutionary creativity as a whole being. You want that. Feel yourself asking for this power one hundred percent—and saying *Yes*—when God gives it to you.

Yes, I accept. Yes, I express. The highest pleasure is the pleasure of power.

I'm feeling the tremendous pleasure of power. Let's feel it together. Is it pleasurable for the *power for*, the *power over* and the *power of* to be expressed through you as the power of love itself? Is that pleasurable? Could there be a higher pleasure than that? It's pleasure all the way through.

The highest power is to act and surrender in the same moment.

To act and surrender in the same moment is not possible as an individuated, separated self.

What's acting and surrendering is the impulse of creation as me doing this, totally one hundred percent. The highest power is to act and surrender in the same moment. Let's see if we can access that ourselves, individually, to act with this tremendous power of expression in all its forms and surrendering to the greater Impulse of Evolution or God within us creating at one time.

They are inseparable. You can't do one without the other. Inaction, in action.

The inaction is the part in me that is sourcing. Action in inaction is: *I'm holding the entire source of creation from the deepest inner essence, expressing uniquely as me and you and us.*

To deny your full power is to deny God.

To deny your full power, your full expression, your full creativity, your full yearning and heart desires is to deny the power of God as you creating.

To deny your full power is to stand against the Good, the True and the Beautiful.

So, to accept my full power is to stand with the Good, the True and the Beautiful the whole way.

Do you see the glorious presence that each of us is when we do this? Wow. Can you feel yourself so glorious? Can you see how when you say hello to somebody, you are communicating this power and the person is turned on? Can you feel yourself? I am the Good, the True and the Beautiful in person as an expression of God. Transformation into all of this is the highest form of power.

THE POWER OF *DHARMA*: THE INNER PHYSICS OF REALITY

When we say that the codes are *dharma,* sometimes people get confused as to what we mean, so let me say what we mean by *dharma.* Everyone has their own gorgeous, unique place in the world and their own unique value—that is one way of using the word *dharma.* Here, *dharma* means something very specific. *Dharma* **means that we have spent a few decades, and we are completely committed, and we have tried to work out the nature of Reality.** You wouldn't go into a physics class and say to the physicist, *everyone in the physics class has their physics theory because we take physics theory seriously.* No, the physicist has worked hard alongside other physicists to get the theory as accurate as possible. *Dharma* **is the interior physics of Reality**.

39

Barbara has been studying and teaching Conscious Evolution for 40 years and that's a gorgeous *dharma*. It is worked out. It has a lot of science behind it, both interior science and exterior science. That's a *dharma* that is now merging with these memetic codes and creating a larger integrity.

In the human potential movement or in the New Age movement, we often don't take ourselves seriously. The same way a physics professor wouldn't say, *everyone in the physics class has their own physics theory*, so too I don't think everyone has their own *dharma* per se.

It is more like: if you want to contribute to physics, then what you do is either study physics, or you find a particular place where you want to really invest your energy. You learn it. You master it. You make it yours, and then perhaps you even contribute to advancing it.

That is the way to step into *dharma*. **Dharma** **means the best integration of premodern, modern, and postmodern thought—integrated together (sciences, anthropology, mathematics, the Great Traditions)—to create right sentences that reflect Reality.**

So, when we write a code, we don't just write the code. That code is a product of the best thinking we can find and integrate in body, heart, and mind over decades. We swallow it whole and then put it back into a formula that you can access and clearly understand. That is what *dharma* is, and it is the core of the church.

Now from that holy place, I want to kind of dive into this kind of gorgeous understanding of power because *dharma* is a form of power. You can think of *dharma* as the mechanism of Conscious Evolution. How does Conscious Evolution work? How does The Universe: A Love Story work? It works through power. What moves in me? What is powerful in me? You always find, in your first person, what's powerful in you.

You are attracted. You are *allured,* which is a word that I always deploy because I like it so much. It says something slightly different:

- You can catch the magic of allurement. It is magical.
- Allurement is primary. It is mystery.
- There is nothing underneath it. I am allured.
- I am allured to come to church.
- I am allured to work on the *dharma*.
- I am allured to dedicate my life to Conscious Evolution. I am allured.
- Allurement is power. I am allured, I am drawn, and that allurement is the most powerful thing moving in me.

That's the beginning. Now, what does allurement do? Allurement is the *power of* that is in the code. The *power of* what? It's the *power of transformation.* **Allurement is the power of transformation.** When quarks are allured, they transform. Allurement is the power. The power of allurement is the power of transformation. And again remember that Eros is radical aliveness seeking ever greater connection and ever greater wholeness.

> *The power of transformation is everything. It means I can change. I am so powerful that I can change. I can transform.*

How do I transform? I am allured to the memory of my future. I am allured to be something more than I am now. I'm drawn towards it. That's such a huge idea. I'm allured to my transformation, and that fills me with power.

When I'm allured to my transformation, I am filled with power.

Take the next step. Just feel the power now.

If I'm not allured to my transformation, and I am not filled with that power of transformation, then the only thing I have left is the superficial version, the pseudo version of *power over*, not genuine power over, which we will get to.

If I am not allured to my transformation and filled with power, the only thing I have left is a pseudo version of *power over* you in the most dominant, dominator sense—in the superficial sense: the task master, the sadist. **Sadism comes from wanting to have power over you, since I am not connected to the power of my own transformation.**

Sadism is not just from of books of eighteenth-century French author, the Marquis de Sade, writing in the Renaissance. Sadism is something that lives in many people. I've seen sadism in some of the greatest teachers. As I got to know them in class, I saw that there's a sadistic streak there. I have seen sadism in CEOs, and I've seen sadism in just about every place. Underneath smiles, there is sadism.

Sadism means, I get my power by lording it over you in some way, and making you vulnerable to me, and playing mind games with you. There are lots of ways to play that sadistic game.

But here's the rule: sadists are not *out there*. Everyone has a little sadist voice in them. Your sadist voice also always comes from, *I am disconnected from the power of my own transformation.* **The second I'm allured to my transformation and am filled with authentic power, all sadism disappears**—instead I'm filled with fierce, quivering tenderness and love.

Do you get that? It is huge. So, we start with the *power of*.

---

*It is the power of transformation: I am
allured to the memory of my future.*

First, I have allurement. The interior quality of allurement is love. I am driven towards deeper and deeper intimacy with myself and with all of Reality.

When I am allured to the memory of my future, and I am animated by pleasure, I am driven towards deeper and wider intimacies, and I am filled with power. Then I don't need a superficial pseudo version of *power over*; my power is *for*, it is *for my highest self.*

It is the power for service. So that is the *power of*, and that is *power for*.

THE MYSTERY OF DIVINE INCARNATION: *POWER OVER* IS ALSO HOLY

Now, let's go the last step.

Now we understand that *power of* is the power of transformation, which is energized by allurement.

Think about it for a second. There's always the image of the man or the woman in the great fable, in the mystery tale, who hears about a beautiful man or a beautiful woman across the sea. They are powered by this incredible allurement, and even though there are *lions and tigers and bears, oh my*, nothing stops them from slaying dragons. They will do anything to meet the great wizard, or the great man or woman.

It's allurement. Allurement is what drives us. I'm filled with the power of transformation and the little hidden sadist voice disappears.

> *The second I'm filled with power,*
> *I stop playing power games.*

The superficial power games disappear—I don't need to destroy someone. I don't need to launch crusades. When Christianity launched its tragic crusades, it was because Christianity had lost the power of transformation. And you know why? Because Christianity said, *you only have grace through Christ.* That is a crazy disaster. If you only have grace through Christ, that means you are not engaged in transformation anymore. Just by believing in Christ, you are saved. That's it. That's the whole story: Christianity abandoned transformation.

In its formal doctrine, and it was only in the past few hundred years since the Renaissance, Christianity has been trying to reclaim transformation. When you abandon transformation, you start sadistic crusades because the only thing you have is *power over*. You don't have the *power of*, which is the power of transformation. The genuine power of transformation is when I offer up my transformation because *I am evolution*.

That's the credo of Evolutionary Church: *I am evolution*. So, my transformation is the transformation of the whole story. **The allurement arising in me is the allurement of evolution itself.**

Evolution is seeking to transform through my transformation. But if I transform someone else's transformation, it simply doesn't work. I could be living my whole life and be ostensibly powerful and public and doing these great things and writing books and yet have blown my whole life.

You know why? It wasn't *my* transformation. You have to know what your transformation is to do. Your transformation means you must access your optimum point of discomfort. It cannot be so discomforting that you are knocked out of the game. You can hold your space, but there is an optimum point of discomfort that is your transformation. Ask yourself, *what is my transformation to do?*

Why do we need *power over* at all? It is a big deal. Why do we need *power over*? **We need *power over* because the ultimate transformation is when we realize that we all do have power over each other.** Of course we do.

The deepest teachings of the erotic mystics—of the great sages in Kashmir Shaivism, *Kabbalah*, and Sufism—got this in a really deep way: **when infinite Reality created the manifest world, infinite Reality said—and this is the deepest understanding of the Christ idea—God said, *I love you so much, I am prepared to need you.***

Christ said, *I love you so much, I need you to redeem me from the cross. I love you so much that if you don't find your way and find that Christ voice in your heart, that God voice in your heart, if you are not allured to your own transformation, then something in me, something in an infinite God dies.*

God, who is the Infinity of Power, will step back and say, *I am going to contract my power and give you, human being, power over me.*

That is the mystery of incarnation, right there:

Infinite Power said, I am going to contract my power to give you power over me.

That is the mystery of Conscious Evolution. The mystery of Conscious Evolution and the mystery of incarnation are the same. The mystery of Conscious Evolution is that God stepped back and said:

- I am going to give you power over me.
- I love you so madly that I trust you.
- I am going to surrender my power to you.
- God says to the human being, *I can't do it without you.*
- That is the mystery.
- That is the mystery of incarnation.
- That is the mystery of Conscious Evolution.

Is that not amazing? It's the same mystery. Do you get that? So, we have power over each other. That is the structure of Reality, and when we don't really get that we have authentic power over each other, we try and exert superficial, tyrannical, sadistic, manipulative power over each other. In truth, we need each other desperately—and not in a codependent way. We are utterly intertwined. **All power is one power. All these three faces of**

authentic power are one. This is the Holy Trinity. These are the three faces of the one.

We say, I am stepping back because I love you so madly, and I can't do it without you. Without merging memes, I can't do it. Without joining genius, I can't do it. I can't do it myself. None of us can do it ourselves, but we can do it together. That is where the power is, the power of Unique Self Symphony.

We sometimes call it a "Planetary Pentecost." It is the Unique Self Symphony. It is the *Planetary Awakening in Love through Unique Self Symphony* where we realize we need all the instruments, and we can do it together.

It is the *dharma* of Reality itself: I can't do it without you, but we sure can do it together.

We sure can do it together!

CHAPTER FOUR

THE LOVE OF POWER AND THE POWER OF LOVE

Episode 114 — December 22, 2018

EVOLUTIONARY LOVE CODE: WE ALL HAVE POWER OVER EACH OTHER

As we go into our code, I want to just remind us all about power. We speak here of the power of love to evolve the world. We are living in a moment where the misuse of power for the very first time ever can destroy the entire species quickly because we never had power of the degree of destructiveness that we now have.

We cannot just depend on a mild form of loving power. This church is activating evolutionary power for the first time at this scale. Let's think not only of how we are going to evolve power to represent this divine elixir of power, but we are going to deal with the power that could destroy our entire species in about ten minutes.

> Our narrative of power is directly emergent from our narrative of identity, which is directly emergent from our Universe Story. Power is a divine elixir, nectar, and a not poison.

There are three forms of power. The first two forms of power are *power over* and *power for*. Contrary to the popular understanding which deifies *power for* and demonizes *power over*, both forms of power are holy.

The third form of power is the *power of*. All three forms of power are inextricable from each other: three faces of one.

Love and power are not opposites. The love of power is inseparable from the power of love.

The Outrageous Lover is power-hungry. The highest pleasure is the pleasure of power. The highest power is to act and surrender in the same moment—Inaction in action, action in inaction. To deny your full power is to deny God.

To deny your full power is to stand against the Good, the True and the Beautiful.

We are on the most awesome, powerful, wild, ecstatic, wondrous day! It's Barbara's birthday! Oh my God, it is Barbara's birthday. Your birthday is the day God said, *I cannot do it without your power*. The whole *dharma* is literally in a birthday.

But what does Barbara's birthday really mean?

It's unbelievable that literally God is the Infinity of Power and that Infinity of Power at a particular moment in time intended Barbara Marx Hubbard-ness, and turned to Barbara Marx Hubbard and said, *Oh my God, meet me in the tomb of Metamorphosis, and I cannot do it without you, even though I am the Infinity of Power.*

If I'm the Infinity of Power, how could it possibly be that I can't do it without you? That's a direct contradiction. Those two things, these sentences, make no sense:

I am God, the Infinity of Power, and I turned to Barbara and I say, *I can't do it without you.*

It makes no sense. I'm the most powerful person ever; but the essence of *I love you* is *I need you*, and *I can't do it without you*. The second Goddess says *I can't do without you*. What Goddess is saying is:

- *I'm limiting my power.*
- *I'm sharing my power with you.*
- *I have the Infinity of Power, and I am empowering you.*

We talk so much about empowerment, but what does empowerment mean? The politically correct world has this little contradiction: it labels power as abusive, but then it sneaks in power on the other side and talks about empowerment. You notice that there is this double move. But actually, if I empower you, then you have power, and I can only empower you if I'm giving you some of my power.

So, for example, to join genius, we have to empower each other to empower each other. We have to say, *I give you power over me*. The way you play, the way you teach, the way you act has power over me. It impacts me, I impact you. We impact each other and we are so powerful that we can surrender. God is so powerful that God can surrender some of God's power to you, and trust that Barbara is going to live the gorgeous Evolutionary Unique Self, *Homo amor*, as Barbara Marx Hubbard, the CosmoErotic Universe in person. That power is going to be powerful.

It is going to be *power over* and it is going to be *power for*.

In the deepest place power over and power for merge together.

In previous weeks, we'd talked about the distinction between *power over* and *power for*. We talked about *power for*, for the service of, in service of, and for the sake of, being the primary sacred form of power.

Then we evolved the *dharma*, we deepened it, and we realized that *power over* is not just a shadow form, but *power over* is a divine elixir. It is a delight! I have *power over* you as a function of love.

My power over you means *I impact you*. We excite each other. We get excited together. We experience vocational evolutionary arousal, and we impact each other.

That's what love means. When I love someone, I say, *you have power over me*, and it means you can hurt me. It means you can blow my heart open. Just by the glance of your delight, I can feel the self-evident goodness of my being alive in the world.

We have power over each other.

A BIRTHDAY TELLS A STORY OF THE POWER OF TRANSFORMATION

A birthday is the beginning of the story of the power of transformation, and my whole life is a series of transformations. Transformation does not stop literally until my last breath. So, **there's no such thing as old or young; there are just deeper and deeper transformations**.

And when you're transforming ever more deeply, you realize that Reality is birthing anew in every moment, and that moments don't repeat. Just like there's a Unique Self of a person, there's a Unique Self of time: every moment is new.

My Unique Self is intended, empowered, and made wildly, ecstatically central and important by Divinity. We have in physics the concept of *multiple centers*. So, Barbara Marx Hubbard is on her birthday, the center of the Universe, empowered by the Infinity of Power.

She doesn't get older; she gets newer every day because she engages in ever deeper transformation. Then when we come together and celebrate that birth—and when we together birth *Homo amor*—there's so much power there.

We birth a church of Evolutionary Love.

When we realize that each of our birthdays is in devotion to birthing the next evolution of the source code—taking us from dystopia, meaning billions of people suffering and possibly dying in the next several decades, to a potential heaven on Earth by enacting a new story of Reality—we realize that God turns to us and says, *I can't do it without you.*

My birthday, Barbara said, *and the birthday of Evolutionary Church—let's make it all one birthday.* Yes, it is all one birthday. Barbara is first, and we are just delighted. We are not only loving Barbara; we are madly loving Barbara.

Hafiz says, *love is for the courtly people, mad love is for us.*

We are madly loving you. We are delighting in you. We are honoring you.

And together with my (Marc's) whole mate, my beloved evolutionary partner, I'm so honored, so delighted to celebrate this birth with you and to birth together with all of us as *Homo amor,* the next stage of human evolution.

When we say that, we are not being grandiose, we are not exaggerating, we are not hyperbolizing. It is true—and to get that will blow your heart so wide open that you'll have a Christmas and a new year that is unimaginable.

Homo amor is the birth of the new Christ. It is the newness that is happening.

THE INFINITY OF POWER SAYS I CAN'T DO IT WITHOUT YOU

Let's take all of that into prayer. Let's take it all before the Infinity of Power, who is also the Infinity of Intimacy.

We celebrate all of our birthdays and the birthday of *Homo amor*, the birthday of the new Christ. We are going to celebrate it now together. We don't bypass our personal stories. You can't go big until you go into the infinite dignity of your story.

Prayer affirms the dignity of personal need, and when we come before God in prayer, we ask for literally everything to manifest:

- For Aunt Sadie's knee operation
- For Uncle Mo's prosperity
- For my health
- For the health of my neighbor
- For everything that the world needs

I ask for everything. You don't leave anything out. I come before the Divine who loves me madly and I share my *holy and my broken Hallelujah*.

I turn to the Infinity of Intimacy and say, *oh my God, I love you. I need you.*

The Infinity of Intimacy turns to you and says, *I love you. I need you. You have power over me. I am going to give you everything I can. Open your hands and receive it.*

Let's pray like we've never prayed before.

Let's pray in a way that we ask for everything. We know our own outrageous beauty and we know that **God as the Infinity of Intimacy said, *I can't do it without you,* and so therefore, I need everything in order to be fully, radically empowered as an agent of the evolutionary awakening, as *Homo amor*, as conscious evolution.**

When you actually say the prayer and write it, something happens and opens in you and opens in the world, and you enter into the mind and heart of God—and things begin to create and manifest. It's real.

SOCIETY'S MISUSE OF POWER LEADS TO TOTAL ANNIHILATION

Since we are approaching Christmas, the birth of the Christ child, it happens to be my (Barbara's) birthday. I always associate my birth with Christmas, which I love, and I want to tell you something awesome about how to apply our power.

I am just reading a book by my own brother-in-law, Daniel Ellsberg. It is called *The Doomsday Machine: Confessions of a Nuclear War Planner*. Dan worked for RAND Corporation[1].

He released the Pentagon Papers and was facing 123 years in prison. He was saved by the fact that President Nixon misused his power by sending his aides to get Daniel's private psychiatric material. Nixon's aides were put in prison, and Nixon resigned. Something happened there with Daniel, and I want to just bring it up in relationship to our narrative of power.

This book tells the awesome story where humanity gains the power of God through nuclear power, wherein it is declared quite clearly that our defense strategy of first strike and response strike—if it should ever be used—leads to the annihilation of our species. This is power.

Humans never had anything like that power. As Daniel is describing it, most of the people working for this are good people who thought for a while that they were helping to defeat the Russians.

While they thought they were helping defeat the Russians, the Russians were helping to defeat us, which means we would annihilate each other. I began to think of our narrative here and our code about how great our power needs to be.

---

1   The RAND Corporation is an American nonprofit global policy think tank, research institute, and public sector consulting firm

WE HAVE TO BE MORE POWERFUL THAN THE POWER THAT COULD DESTROY US

Let's connect this message to our church, which is currently held on Saturday. In the New Testament, on Saturday, Jesus was in the tomb of metamorphosis, which makes it the most interesting day of the three days in the tomb.

On day number one, I have been crucified, I am destroyed, I am dead.

On day number three, I'm arising as a new human, *Homo amor* in person.

What did I do on Saturday to become *Homo amor*?

What did Jesus do on Saturday to appear to Mary as the resurrected Christ—a new human capable of doing what he did?

The power we now have through our understanding of how nature works, particularly in the nuclear realm, leads to the misuse of power which could annihilate the entire species. So, since it's Saturday in the tomb of metamorphosis—wherein the misuse of power could possibly destroy our species quickly—**it's also true, in Saturday in the tomb of metamorphosis, that we're evolving our species into a new human**.

The Church of Saturday and the Church of Evolutionary Love is dedicated to *Homo amor*. So, I want to put on the Doomsday Machine another book called *Homo amor* that would recognize the awesome power that the human species has gained through our brilliant understanding of how nature works.

The same species could do that quickly. Isn't it true that the same species could have the power to become *Homo amor*? As we say in the code, *our narrative of power is directly emergent from our narrative of identity.*

Our identity here is *Homo amor*, which is directly emergent from our Universe Story, and the Universe Story is from the origin of creation to the present: A Love Story.

THE LOVE OF POWER AND THE POWER OF LOVE

How is it a love story? Particle to particle, attracted to particle from quarks to us.

If we are going to become Homo amor in our narrative of power— power is a divine elixir, nectar and not a poison—we have to dare be as powerful as the power that could destroy us times ten.

See, we have to be more powerful. Here we have a power that is so great, and our president of the United States is getting more of it. It used to be just the US and USSR, and now it is nine different countries, including our own in the United States.

Now we know we have *power over* to destroy ourselves, now we know we also have *power over* to create a world in which everyone alive can choose to be more of who they truly are and can choose to become a new human, what we call *Homo amor*. It would be *power over* ourselves—the inner being that we are, the inner impulse of evolution that is in us. *Power over* that is to give birth to who we truly are or otherwise allow it to be misused at this scale.

There are three forms of power. The first two are "power over" and "power for."

We must have *power over* this impulse inside ourselves so that it could be as great as the power that we can misuse. This is really fascinating to me because Dan is writing that most people who are doing this are relatively nice and kind, but then he suddenly notices, in the margin of this book, *oh, the annihilation of our species is our plan!* He hardly dared say this, because if he had, he would be cast out from the lineage of power in which you get to know all this stuff.

So, let's have power over the misuse of power, which is awesome. $E=mc^2$ means it is time to blow up the Universe. We must have *power over that* now— *for love!* That power is the greatest it has ever been, so the *power over* has to be the greatest it has ever been—and even greater.

If you really want to look at it, what would make it possible for people to be planning this annihilation? What happened to power?

Contrary to the popular understanding, which deifies *power for* and demonizes *power over*, both forms of power are holy.

The third form of power is the *power of*, the power of life, love, expression, transformation. We've each been given the power of that we used to attribute to the ancient gods.

Let's add high technology. That is the reason we used to call this *Homo amor universalis*. We have now decided to leave off the *universalis*, and simply call it *Homo amor*, which now includes the high-tech genius. It is not enough just to love; you have to have the power in high tech. If high tech is used by *Homo amor* for love, it will change the entire world.

All three forms of power are inextricable from each other—three faces of one. Love and power are not opposites. The love of power is inseparable from the power of love.

How strong would love need to be to change the situation, which is on the threshold of self-destruction of the entire species? Our society is planning for it and spending lots of money on it. As in our Code, *The love of power is inseparable from the power of love.*

This is how great we have to be:

The Outrageous Lover is power hungry.

I am power hungry with this defense department. I am power hungry in making a plan great enough to use the power, rather than to misuse it. We are not going to do this just by being nice. We are all nice, but that is not it: *the Outrageous Lover is power hungry.*

I am power hungry, and I'm inviting everybody to be power hungry. The highest pleasure is the pleasure of power.

I said at Sunrise Ranch[2] the other night, *what is Sunrise Ranch going to do about this 'Doomsday machine'?* The response was, nobody ever thought they had to do anything about it. *We're all going along how nice and how good we are.* I said, *No! I am going to have a meeting at Sunrise Ranch, and I am going to ask everybody what we can do.* Because if we don't feel we are powerful enough to change the course of history—that in our own government and nine others is going to hell—then there's going to be a mistake.

There almost was a mistake during the Cuban Missile Crisis; it almost blew us up, and Khrushchev[3] was able to stop it. He saw it, and he was able to convince the Presidium in Russia that it didn't matter, because all they wanted is to look powerful. When Khrushchev pulled Russia out of the Cuban Missile Crisis, he said the fear was that Russia would lose its prestige. The use of power here is not just simply *power over*, but the *power of being greater than.*

The highest pleasure is the pleasure of power.

The highest power is to act and surrender in the same moment.

Let's act to take this power and then surrender. Wow!

Inaction in action. Action in inaction.

---

2   *Sunrise Ranch, located in Loveland, Colorado, is the headquarters for Emissaries of Divine Light, a global spiritual network. Barbara Marx Hubbard lived there for a period of time.*

3   Nikita Sergeyevich Khrushchev was First Secretary of the Communist Party of the Soviet Union from 1953 to 1964, and Chairman of the Council of Ministers from 1958 to 1964.

To deny your full power is to deny God.

This is true, because if we humans allow our Defense Department, our military, to own the power of science and technology and threaten to destroy the world, we are not using our power right. This is real power that is needed.

To deny your full power is to stand against the Good, the True, and the Beautiful.

If we want the church to become the most powerful church of Evolutionary Love that it needs to be to write together and enact *Homo amor* as the response to the doomsday machine, we can only do it if we have power.

- The greatest power we have in the world today is the power of transformation.
- The highest pleasure is the pleasure of power.
- The highest pleasure of power is the power of transformation.
- The highest transformation is to tell a new story, because the most important thing we need today in the world is a story, one that evolves the source code of culture and consciousness.

It is not enough, as we said, to be nice; I have to be infinitely more powerful than the abuses of power. **The way to be infinitely more powerful than the abuses of power is to access the source code of Reality, and rewrite the code of our culture.** We rewrite the code of our culture through telling a new story, and through the writing of the Evolutionary Love Codes.

It is the single most powerful act that a human being can do at this moment in time, because at every stage of history, they rewrote the source code of culture. We moved out of premodernity to the Renaissance.

CODES OF CULTURE THROUGHOUT HISTORY

Premodernity had codes of culture owned by different cultures: every religion said, our system is the code of culture, and when Reality triumphs, everyone is going to come around and be Christian, or everyone is going to come around and be Islamic, or everyone is going to come around and be Jewish, or Buddhist. Everyone was waiting for their code of culture to triumph.

Then we got to **modernity**, and we said, we can't just be obedient to God, who we think commanded us to make our code of culture triumph. For all the good that those codes had, we needed to place the human being at center stage. And so modernity unpacked a whole bunch of new stories, and those new stories all had science at the core, which was beautiful, but they had many different expressions.

One story was **modern imperialism**—British empire, French empire—that said, *we are going to conquer in the name of our vision.* That didn't work. By the end of World War I, we had realized that imperialism was actually oppressive and brutal, the British Empire was wildly destructive, and people deserved to self-govern. So, imperialism didn't work.

We tried **fascism**—Mussolini, Hitler—with the strongmen stories of modernity. It didn't work. Then we had two stories left. At the dawn of World War I, we had imperialism and fascism, and by the end of World War II, these modern stories had died. We were left with two stories, two global visions: Communism and liberal democracy. There was this huge clash between them.

Communism exploded and fell apart: the supermarket turned out to be more powerful than the gulag. The communist story disappeared, and we were left with one story: liberal democracy.

Now, **liberal democracy** isn't holding. The old vision of liberal democracy is not holding: a million people commit suicide a year, then there's Brexit, and Trump... Liberal democracy is actually saying, *We don't want to be a global vision. Let's take care of ourselves. Let's get out of Syria, let's leave Syria* *to whoever, or who cares what happens there.* Jim Mattis[4] resigned because liberal democracy turned away from its leadership role in the world.

It's a big deal: **liberal democracy doesn't have a narrative of identity, it doesn't have a Universe Story, and it doesn't have a narrative of power, so it doesn't know what to do with its power.**

It's confused about how to exercise its power. It doesn't have a story. The story of liberal democracy we no longer think is the triumphant story that will conquer the world. It is falling apart. Look at the mortgage crisis from 2008. The whole system is fragile, and it's lacking courage. When Vladimir Putin looks at liberal democracy, you know what he sees is missing? For all of Putin's evil, and Putin has genuine evil, he doesn't see their courage, he doesn't see their honor, and he doesn't see this sense of passion. And he's not all wrong. In other words, **what is the vision that liberal democracy is standing for?**

Liberal democracy, for all of its problems, is the best system we have ever had: but we have to invest liberal democracy with a higher vision of democracy and with a vision of who we are. *Homo amor* needs to meet liberal democracy, and a new narrative of power needs to meet liberal democracy.

It needs a new narrative of identity, a new narrative of community, a new Universe Story.

What we are holding in the Church of Evolutionary Love is the set of narratives which have courage, honor, duty, obligation, and the joy of responsibility.

---

4   Jim Mattis is an American military veteran who served as the 26th United States secretary of defense from 2017 to 2019. A retired Marine Corps four-star general, he commanded forces in the Persian Gulf War, the War in Afghanistan, and the Iraq War

We started this by saying that on her birthday, God turns to Barbara and says, *I can't do it without you*. It is not a joke when we say that the Infinity of Power stepped back and said, *you are my partner*. That is the most serious thing. Can you imagine that? That is the most joyous thing we could possibly say, to actually realize I am needed by All-That-Is, and I need to be powerful.

How do we activate this in a real way?

The way we've chosen is to bring together the Foundation for Conscious Evolution, and the Center for Integral Wisdom, and found together the Church of Evolutionary Love. The Church is our vehicle for sharing the codes of the world. Our vision of the Church is there has to be millions, if not hundreds of thousands, of Evolutionary Churches around the world— let's be power hungry.

My colleague Yuval Harari wrote a number of books, which I've talked about a lot about in the last two years, about the desperation and dystopia. We have been talking about this new story, but not the new story in the abstract way Brian Swimme writes about it in his book *The Universe Story*, which basically tells the story of *science is poetic*. I love Brian, but that is not enough.

- ◆ Evolutionary Love drives Reality.
- ◆ I am a unique configuration of Evolutionary Love.
- ◆ We come together as Unique Self Symphony.

We awaken in the self-organizing Universe. **We are the carriers of the codes of culture.** It's not that *someone else is going to do it*. This is ours to do.

In *The Doomsday Machine*, Daniel Ellsberg got this beautiful sense of what went wrong, but he can't quite vision what it means to claim power because he only sees the demonization of power. He doesn't see *Homo amor* and the possibility of *Homo amor*. *Homo amor* is not one person acting in the power structure of Washington. *Homo amor* is literally a self-organizing

Universe arising. It is an uprising the likes of which has never been seen before.

So, let's claim our power. Let's claim our power wildly. Let's claim our power in ways that are unimaginable!

I (Barbara) was speaking with Daniel Ellsberg over breakfast, and he said to me, *Barbara, do you think that anything you could do would be effective?* I could see he didn't think so. Then I said, *Dan, do you think anything that you do could be effective?* He was writing this book, telling the whole truth here, and he said, no, I don't. How could you possibly think you are going to be effective? I said, *well, you are dealing with the military-industrial complex, and I am at the tip of the tipping point.*

We are the tip of the tipping point.
That is so powerful.

This church stands at the tip of the tipping point of humanity. Everybody on Earth who feels they are also at the tip of the tipping point knows that it will tip in this direction.

We are loving the power, the power of love.

CHAPTER FIVE

HOMO AMOR: INCARNATING THE POWER OF EVOLUTIONARY LOVE

Episode 116 — December 29, 2018

EMBRACING *HOMO AMOR*: THE POWER OF LOVE IN HUMAN EVOLUTION

Let's incarnate *Homo amor* personally. Think of the difference between *Homo neanderthalensis* and *Homo sapiens*. Now consider the difference between *Homo sapiens* and *Homo amor*. As we resonate with this code, let's do it from the perspective of *Homo amor*.

EVOLUTIONARY LOVE CODE: LOVE AND POWER ARE NOT OPPOSITES

> Our narrative of power is directly emergent from our narrative of identity, which is directly emergent from our Universe Story. There is the description of *Homo amor*, directly emergent from the Universe Story, as the Universe Story evolving.
>
> Power is a divine elixir, nectar, and not poison.

There are three forms of power. The first two forms of power are: *power over* and *power for*. As *Homo amor*, contrary to popular understanding, which deifies *power for* and demonizes *power over*, both forms of power are holy if we are *Homo amor*.

The third form of power is the *power of*.

All three forms of power are inextricable from each other, three faces of one.

Love and power are not opposites; the love of power is inseparable from the power of love. The Outrageous Lover is power-hungry. The highest pleasure is the pleasure of power. The highest power is to act and surrender at the same moment.

In action and inaction, to deny your full power is to deny God. To deny your full power is to stand against the good, the true, and the beautiful.

EVOLUTIONARY LOVE: WHAT CHURCH IS MEANT TO BE

So much needs to happen, and we are at the center of it as the first church, community of Evolutionary Love, like the Gospel Church which fuelled the civil rights movement and like the new vision that fuelled the Renaissance. We are, literally, holding the codes of the new culture.

When we think about the obstacles in the way of *Homo amor* coming into the world, we discover a mixture of tears of joy and tears of frustration beyond imagination at the obstacles that are actually blocking *Homo amor*. We know that we're sitting on the codes of the culture, and that we have to deliver them (that is what we were born for). We feel the joy knowing that we have to love each other so deeply to do it.

There is a beautiful Evolutionary Love Code which says, love and power are not opposites. **The love of power is inseparable from the power of love. So, we want to restore integrity to power.**

There are people working with a national political party, trying to increase their political power, and restore integrity and power there. That is important. But if you want to know the power of Evolutionary Church, it is the church of Evolutionary Love. Our power is that we love each other. We don't just love each other; we love each other madly. We do not just say it, or assert it, or declare it—although we do all of them, and that's all important—*but we feel it*. We feel it! What is so beautiful about it is you are able to access the full power of love that lives in the Cosmos, driving everything—every second, and you are blown away.

What we try to practice is to access that inner feeling of Cosmos where we love each other so much and we see each other's beauty. We can feel each other; intimacy: feeling you feeling me. The power is that we love each other so much and we are so committed to this vision, to this mission, to this unfolding of Conscious Evolution as Evolutionary Love, that:

We know we are holding the codes of the culture.

Community is not a detail for us; it's not something we come to get a little fix of something, that we actually say, *this is our community*—not *my* community, not *your* community, not *someone else's* community. It's *our* community. It's not just a place that we affiliate with and belong to—that would be Maslow level 2. No, this is Maslow level 7.[5]

---

5   Abraham Maslow's hierarchy of needs is a psychological theory that outlines a five-tier model of human needs, often depicted as hierarchical levels within a pyramid. The levels are: physiological needs (air, water, food, shelter, clothing, sleep), safety needs (personal security, financial security, health and well-being, safety against accidents and illness), love and belongingness needs (emotional relationships, friendships, family, intimate connections, community), esteem needs (self-respect, independence, achievement, status, recognition, appreciation), and self-actualization needs (realization of potential, self-fulfillment, personal growth, peak experiences). Maslow later expanded the hierarchy to include cognitive, aesthetic, and self-transcendence needs, but the five-tier model remains the most widely recognized.

This is the place. This is the vehicle. This is our *Kabbalah*. In Hebrew mysticism we would say this is our chariot, and with this chariot we can literally turn community around. We can transform it and we can do it; it's a re-coding project within our communities.

We've been *re-coding* culture for over ten years, and people are just now getting it: *Oh, what's the new story?*

We are holding the new story.

We have something audacious, and we stake our lives on it. We have the best vision of the new Universe Story:

- A new narrative of identity
- A new narrative of power
- A new narrative of a sexuality
- A new narrative of relationships
- A new narrative of medicine, education, and entrepreneurship

Do *we* have any idea what that means?

This is not a casual project. **The community of Evolutionary Love, in potential, is the single most potent vehicle.** The churches, synagogues, mosques, and other organizations of Spirit that meet regularly and hold the new codes are the vehicle **that transforms and evolves Reality.**

We are literally standing between dystopia and utopia.

In 20 years, most people in America and around the world are not going to have a narrative of identity that comes from having a job, because you will not have a job. With automation it is going to be an entirely different world. There is going to be an entirely different set of realities.

Our ability to navigate is our ability to not just survive and thrive, but to actually remain on planet Earth—to actually usher in Heaven on Earth, to articulate and live these new codes.

We are what we are holding. It is so precious, and it is in every note we write. It is how we talk to each other, and the key and power is here. The key and power here is the greatest power in the world. The greatest power in the world is God's power and relationship to us, which means:

God has all the power. God does not need us, but God feels us and loves us madly. So when we become God, it means we have all the power—power over you: I love you; I need you. I have power over you, but we do not abuse that power, not even subtly.

It's not a micro-aggression. Instead, we micro-love. A billion moments of micro-love, those little details of love, all contain the power of Evolutionary Love that drives all of Reality. When we say good morning, in that, we want to feel all of the love of all of Reality. In every word, the words are all perfect. Every time you type, let the Outrageous Love—the Evolutionary Love that actually initiated and animates Cosmos—move through your fingers, so that in every note you or someone reads, you get this transmission and you are blown away. Your heart is blown open.

- You fall beside your small stuff.
- There's no game.
- There are no power games.

The greatest power is to surrender to each other's beauty, in mad love, and in mad devotion. Sometimes it is so precious. We have to love each other.

We stop loving each other when we get insulted. In every fight we feel insulted because we feel like we are not being seen. We feel like our gorgeousness is not witnessed. Let's witness each other's gorgeousness.

*The opposite of an insult?
Microdoses of mad outrageous
Evolutionary Love. That's power.*

We come before God who does not need us at all, and God says, *I love you madly.* In the entire infinity of God's power, the infinity of Divine power, comes the Infinity of Intimacy; and love and power, are not opposites—they are interwoven with each other.

When we bring our holy and broken *Hallelujahs* (or prayers) before God, we pour it all out, and we ask for everything. **We're reclaiming prayer and in the Church of Evolutionary Love prayer affirms dignity**—personally. We recognize that God is the Infinity of Power, but the inside of that power is intimacy.

So, you cannot just ask for peace in the world; you have to ask for everything you need and know that the Infinity of Intimacy holds it. God/Goddess knows everything that we want and desperately wants to meet that, just as we want to meet each other.

One of the things we are trying to reclaim is a vision of God that both lives in me and as me. God is the third-person force of Evolutionary Love and creativity that drives Cosmos, but God is also second-person. Rumi said, *I fall into the arms of the beloved.* So, when we turn to the Divine we articulate the very depth of our need.

Let's take our prayers and lift them to the sky—lift them up and transform them to bring down the codes of culture.

Let's do that together, and love each other madly, with radical delight.

INCARNATING *HOMO AMOR*: EMBRACING COLLECTIVE POWER AND LOVE

We are directing a prayer for the very first time to all of us, through all of us as *Homo amor.* We are experiencing this code, which we will re-read, and we see that *Homo amor* resides in us collectively. Unless *Homo amor* resides in us collectively, it will not reside in us individually. We cannot be a new species if we are walking around without others. We are going to read this as *Homo amor*, and we are going to speak as *Homo amor*. Then we will talk about how we act truly incarnated.

Here is the first part of the Code again:

> Our narratives of power, your narrative, my narrative, our narrative of power, directly emerges from our narrative of identity...

Feel the new identity that we are as *Homo amor*.

The next line of the code:

> ...that we are directly emergent from our Universe Story.

What does that really mean to be directly emergent from our Universe Story? Take a perspective of the billions of years of evolution as a spiral. Look at the core of the spiral as allurement (in Wheel 2.0). Bring the impulse of allurement that is guiding the Universe Story directly into your heart as your impulse of allurement, empowered with the impulse of creation.

> Power is a divine elixir and not poison.

> There are three forms of power. The first two forms of power are *power over* and *power for*. Then there is *power of*.

Take them all as incarnating the impulse of evolution coming from Source, from Spirit, from the mind of God, through the Big Bang, through the incredible genius from a single cell, to multi-cell, to animal, to human, to you, and me incarnating the power of Universe: A Love Story.

> Contrary to the popular understanding that deifies *power for* and demonizes *power over*, both forms of power are sacred.

You, I, and we are expressions of the universal impulse of creation. That impulse has direction toward more love, more creativity, and more genius—that power is within us.

By recognizing and embracing this power, we are sanctifying our own expression of it. This power allows us to both fully express who we are, and become a part of, and lover of everyone else doing the same. Only through love of each other, Outrageous Love, Evolutionary Love, can any one of us incarnate the awesome nature of this power.

If you try to do it all by yourself alone, you will not make it.

But if you feel you are part of the Field, which is itself arising from the whole Universe story through every one of us uniquely, then our prayers are the power of the Universe praying. You are not praying all by yourselves. Even though it is totally personal, it is totally cosmic.

We can pray almost constantly and here is a way to do it.

Feel the impulse of evolution personalized as your intention, your passion, your longing, your love, your problems, and all the things that we cannot figure out. Then stop and ask that impulse as God itself within. We could be taking a walk and talking out loud:

Dear God, what shall I do about X to realize the full implication of Your intention in me?

Dear God, I don't quite know how to do this, could you please tell me?

I am talking to you now, dear God.

Dear God, show me exactly how to respond to any crisis any of us might be facing now.

Dear God, given the direction of evolution towards more consciousness, more freedom, more complexity, more love, Dear God, what is the exact microcosmic way for me to respond to this?

This is where it is in the details of how you respond. But, how do you know how to respond if you are facing something that you do not have a good answer for?

I find that God knows what I should do—not like saying *you need to do this or that*, but because the inner impulse of the Divine knows how to respond to X-, Y-, or Z-crisis, or -difficulty, or to somebody I would like to hit over the head. I love, then, for God to reveal the way forward in the details, in case I don't know the way forward in any detail I am facing right now.

Take a moment to ask God collectively, but let's do it personally first. Find whatever it is that might be the most challenging. We personalize our asking like this:

Dear God, as the impulse of evolution in me, as the genius of the entire story of creation as me... (Because who else? What is going to be affected but us?)

Then the genius evolution starts to reveal itself to you, to me. Then I write it in my journal. This is another thing: I write it down because it is so precious, but it is also evanescent. So, let's say you get a really great message from God to solve a unique crisis you are facing. It is sometimes called an epiphany, like an A-ha! *Oh, of course God, this would be the best way.* Usually it demonstrates love and creativity; it does not hit somebody and kill them. If anything, it actually empowers them.

Then I repeat it out loud and say, *thank you, God, I see, I got it.* We could just talk to ourselves on a walk. *Hey God, that is so brilliant!* Then I get home, and I write it down. And I have a journal full of these epiphanies! And I tell you, if you live your life that way—it is all there!

As *Homo amor* I ask,

Dear God, what is the best thing that Homo amor, as a small group, can do to release the love, the creativity, and the genius, upon this planet in time to avoid devolution and extinction?

What I am getting is I sense God saying that we can all recognize the codes inside ourselves. You can ask exactly how to respond to *exactly* what you are facing. Let God reveal it. Then share it with your journal, and

71

possibly one other who will receive it with all the feelings of tenderness and vulnerability.

Find someone that you could share exactly what God told you when it really hurts—it might be embarrassing for you to even reveal it. Through that acceptance of God and the shared field of two or more, you have a resonant field. Then bring it into the community, the largest resonant field of Evolutionary Love we know on Earth. When you pray it in community, it becomes more than prayer all by yourself on a walk or even with one other person.

HOW DO WE CONTRIBUTE TO THIS LOVE?

We contribute to this exact frequency of prayer personally, socially and collectively. What contribution can you make, can I make, can we make—to bring this to the world in time for the planetary awakening to happen, rather than de-evolution and extinction? That is important.

HOMO AMOR: EMBRACING OUR UNIQUE EVOLUTIONARY LOVE

Homo amor! Let's pick up this word, this beautiful and holy word: *Homo amor*. I (Marc) remember the feeling when that word first came down. I was just feeling the pain of Reality, and asking what needs to happen next?

And then this word—*Homo amor* just came into existence, and we infused it and worked with that word—it was *Homo amor universalis* for a while. We eventually settled on *Homo amor*.

Homo amor incorporates everything—all of the technological, high-tech potential power—but we invest that power with that which will turn it from devolution to evolution.

Who are we? Let's go back to the very basic. Who is *Homo amor*?

Homo amor is the genus—the new humanity.

- ◆ Each of us is *Homo amor in person.*
- ◆ We are the Cosmic Universe *in person.*
- ◆ We are Conscious Evolution *in person.*

Every time we micro-love or we microdose the world with love, that is the evolutionary impulse showing up through us. We are the micro-impulses of evolution poured into Reality. So how do we know? How do we know what to do?

We need two things. First: *Who am I? Who are you?* Let's find our place, let's rework, let's find who you are. Let's set in a new way:

You are an irreducibly unique expression of the LoveDesire, the LoveIntelligence, and the LoveBeauty of All-That-Is, micro-loving, micro-pulsing in you, as you, and through you, that never was, is, or will be ever again—other than through you. And as such, you stand on the abyss of darkness, facing a particular dimension of un-love in the world. It is only your micro-pulses of Evolutionary Love that could stand on that abyss and say, *Let there be light.*

It's only your unique frequency of light that can light up the darkness in a particular place in your heart, and the heart of Reality, in a way that no one who ever was, is, or will be can ever do—other than through you.

As such, you realize: Oh my Goddess, we have an irreducible unique perspective and we have an irreducible unique quality of intimacy, which gives and manifests and fosters my capacity to give my unique gifts of micro-impulses of Evolutionary Love.

Now there's only one question we have to ask. There is no other question I ever have to ask in the world:

---

*Dear God, what is it that You,
evolution, the evolutionary God, need
from me in the very next moment?*

That is the only question I ever have to ask. Then I listen for the answer.

Let's actually pray together:

Dear God/Goddess,

What do you need from me as Homo amor, in person, that

NO ONE ELSE that ever was, is, or will be, can do other than me?

What do you need from me today?

Just that phrase, nothing else. Can you feel it?

As *Homo amor* in person, the first step is that we must unguard our hearts.

Because I want to know what love is, and we need each other. That is the first step and a really important step. *Imagine that every single person on the planet says I am going to unguard my heart.*

We are so armored.

I am going to unguard my heart.

Let's blast it open.

That is our prayer that we pray every day: *I unguard my heart. All my heartache, all my pain. Homo amor!*

We are doing this not just for ourselves, we are literally evolving the source code of love as *Homo amor* in person.

Feel the prayer lifting as *Homo amor* in person.

The phrase *that no one else...* that is a huge one. That is audacious. You have to understand what it means: *that no one else can do this.*

We then realize *I am irreplaceable*—no one else. Those are pretty awesome words, those are pretty audacious words, but that is actually the truth of the interior face of the Cosmos.

CHAPTER SIX

EMBRACING OUR COSMIC SIGNIFICANCE

Episode 117 — January 5, 2019

EVOLUTIONARY LOVE CODE: ARE YOU READY?

Are you ready to play a larger game?

Are you ready to be evolution?

Are you ready to participate in the evolution of culture and consciousness?

Are you ready to participate in the evolution of love?

Are you ready to love deeper and wider than you ever have before?

Are you ready to include something or someone in your circle of love that has always been on the outside?

Are you ready to change, grow and transform in a way that you have long ago given up on?

Are you ready to be and become more than you ever thought possible?

Are you ready to be a dreamer?

Are you ready to activate Evolutionary Love, in you, as you and through you?

Are you ready to awaken as Conscious Evolution?

WE ARE THE CHOSEN ONES

We have this enormous sense of possibility. We are pregnant—with an *orgia*[6] of joined genius, with an ecstasy of joined genius, with an ecstasy of passion and compassion—as we realize that we are the ones, that we are the delighted ones.

We are the chosen ones.

When we say we are the chosen ones we do not mean it in the old way, like we are chosen and therefore we are better. The experience of being chosen is the fundamental experience of the Unique Self. It is to know that I am *chosen.*

One of the six core realizations of the Unique Self is to know that *I am chosen.* Not only are we chosen individually but this Unique Self Symphony, which is our community, is chosen.

- We are chosen to play a larger game.
- We are chosen to look beyond the petty contractions of where we have been insulted.
- We are chosen even to look beyond the important personal work that we have all done and continue to do, because the personal work never stops. It is always necessary, and we are in that so deeply.

We are now shifting our personal work for the sake of evolution. We are realizing that we are activated as evolution. We've been saying, as my

---

6   Often meaning orgy, the word from Latin is used to mean an act of frenzied or immoderate indulgence.

teacher Abraham Kook said, *ha'sodot hem b'tochenu*[7]—*I am evolution*. Oh my God! The mysteries are within us. It is what we call—a new word that I made up about a week and a half ago—the anthro-ontological experience.

Anthro is like in *anthropocentric*—*anthro*, a human being. Ontology means it is *for realsies*. Remember that word? *For realsies* is not a precise translation of ontology, which is concerned with the nature of being or the kinds of things that have existence, but it will work.

Ontology means it is not made up, it is not a social construction, it is for real, it is an ultimate issue. We are evolution, for real. *I am evolution* is an anthro-ontological statement. It is not a metaphor. It is not poetry. It is the very prose of Reality.

As Kook writes, *the mysteries are within us. My eye is the eye of evolution. Not only, I am evolution but I am Evolutionary Love. Not only am I Evolutionary Love but I am a unique configuration of Evolutionary Love.*

The questions we're asking ourselves: Are we ready to play a larger game? Are we ready to be evolution?

Are we ready to participate in the evolution of love?

The reason Donald Trump got elected as president of the United States is because Barack Obama, Hillary Clinton, and liberal democracy itself lost its vision and lost its Universe Story.

Liberal democracy (which was basically free markets), and participatory classical democracy (in all of its beauty and open borders), and this liberal idea of *let's get educated by reading literature*—**these are not enough because they are not rooted in a Universal Story.**

 ♦   These do not birth a narrative of identity.

---

7   Rabbi Abraham Isaac Kook, *Orot HaKodesh*, Volume 2, Section 351.

- ◆ They do not have a narrative of power.
- ◆ They do not have a sexual narrative.
- ◆ They do not have a narrative of relationship out of which emerges a narrative of entrepreneurship and of medicine and of education and of science and of recovery .

What is the story that we need to tell?

ARE WE READY TO DREAM GOD'S DREAM?

It's not about the best made-up story, not the best metaphor, but the best, most grounded story and the deepest wisdom. I call this the exterior and the interior sciences. We have to be rooted in natural law, but natural law is not only the law of the exterior sciences. Natural law is also the law of the interior sciences.

When we pray we turn to God, to the God who holds us and knows our name—not just to the superficial, narcissistic New Age adaption in the thought that *I am God*. Slow down. Let God hold you. Let God hold me. Let's rest in the Divine like Rumi[8] and Hafiz did—the Divine who's the Infinity of Intimacy, who knows my name and holds me, and who holds my holy and my broken *Hallelujah*.

But that is not enough. I need to get beyond the narcissistic adaption and get to the deep truth that I am God. **The God who holds me also participates in me and lives in me, as me, and through me** as the last line of our code says, *I am ready to be activated as Evolutionary Love.* This

---

8   Rumi, whose full name is Jalal al-*Din* Muhammad Rumi, was a thirteenth-century Persian poet, Islamic scholar, theologian, and Sufi mystic. Born on September 30, 1207, in Balkh (now in Afghanistan) and later settling in Konya (present-day Turkey), Rumi became one of the most influential poets and spiritual masters in history. Hafiz, also known as Hafez, is the pen name of Shams al-*Din* Muhammad, a fourteenth-century Persian poet who is considered one of the greatest masters of Persian lyrical poetry, particularly in the form of the *ghazal*. Born around 1315 in Shiraz, Persia (modern-day Iran), Hafiz is renowned for his poetic expressions of love, mysticism, and the divine.

means to realize, anthro-ontologically that my deepest dreams for healing and transformation are God's dreams.

- Are we ready to dream God's dreams, friends?
- Are we ready to dream the dreams of She?
- Are we ready to dream the dreams of Goddess?

That is what we mean when we ask, *Are you ready to be a dreamer? Are you ready to be activated?*

There are many of us who write Outrageous Love Letters. It is a practice. Maybe thirty or forty people write to each other. One beautiful person wrote me an Outrageous Love Letter the other day, and it went like this:

We are not trivial. We are willing to encounter our cosmic significance.

I said, *Wow!* This person understands the *dharma*. I was ecstatic when I read it.

I want to say it again, the essence of this code: **We are not trivial!**

We are willing to encounter our cosmic significance. That's what this is about.

So, we turn to God who knows our name, who holds us, who is more personal than the most personal moment of romantic love that you can possibly imagine. This is infinitely more intimate and personal than even that, and yet She lives in us.

We bring before Her, in community, our holy and our broken *Hallelujahs*:

Every moment of our lives
Every moment of breakdown
Every moment of despair
Every moment of hurt

Every moment of joy
Every moment of breakthrough

Then we lay them down, as a great Sufi said, *on Her altar.* She holds us and embraces us and receives our prayer and breathes possibility through us.

We are going to pray together. We are going to ask for everything and ask for whatever we need—the deepest things, and the simplest things.

Prayer is personal and affirms the dignity of personal needs.

Let's pray for everything.
Pray for yourself.
Love yourself madly—*I am evolution!*—it is so powerful.

Amen, amen.

EVOLVING A CULTURE OF LOVE AS EVOLUTION IS GOING TOWARD ITS OWN GOAL

One day I asked God, *what can I do to tell the story of Christ as well as you told it in the Bible?*

And I got back: *Tell the story of the birth of humanity as one body, able to heal the Earth, free the people and explore the Universe!*

That became my mission in the world—to go tell that story.

I am evolution. You are evolution. It is such an awesome reality that starts before the Big Bang.

Starting from the origin of creation we are starting up already coded with first of all, the entire story of evolution that made you from quarks, cells, multi-cells, animals. You are all of those things. But now go into the inner impulse of evolution, the self-organizing genius at the interior of evolution. It is *not just the exterior*—billions of years. What happened *inside* those years turns on the spiral to:

+ Led to life

- Led to animal life
- Led to human life
- Led to us becoming *evolutionary* human life
- Led to us becoming a new human, us becoming *Homo amor*

The seriousness of it is that *I am,* and *you are,* coded with the genius that built the Universe. That genius shows up uniquely as each one of us, particularly if we activate our heart's desire.

This is really a lovely thought, that the *I am evolution* inside of you responds most deeply to your deepest heart's desire for the fulfillment of that genius which is each of us drawing on the full potentiality of a whole system of universal evolution, of which every one of us is a unique part.

So, let's take that in as we look at the code.

I am evolution. I am an expression of the impulse of creation with the genius that created the entire Universe inside me, uniquely. This really is the question: What kind of impulse are we willing to express? How far are we ready to go?

Let's hold this code of evolution as the impulse for the billions and billions of years that made the trillions of cells in our bodies—our eyes, our ears, everything—now ready now to say *Yes!* to you, if you say *Yes!* to the whole system.

Are you ready to play a larger game?

If you are taking seriously that you are evolution in person and you are being asked, *Hi Evolution, are you ready to play a larger game, Ms. or Mr. Evolution? Are you?*

Well, if you say, *No,* do you know what happens? You put a lid on the impulse that is you because **the impulse in you and me and every one of us, not only is ready to play the larger game, but that is all that it ever does. Evolution is always evolving into more.**

So, are you ready to play a larger game? What does that feel like? For me:

- It is the planetary awakening in love with the Unique Self Symphony. That is my larger game.
- It is a greeting to the Universe which is undoubtedly filled with life.

Second, are you ready to be evolution? Look into yourself now.

My larger game is the planetary awakening. Go into your larger game and see if you are ready to be evolution, to play it.

Sometimes when I wake up in the morning I say, *I am not ready to play this larger game. I have a cold today; I do not feel well.* Am I willing to play the larger game? Well, you know what has happened by saying *Yes?* I cannot feel the cold anymore. I am not sure that illness can stay in you for long if you say *Yes!* to the larger game and ready to be evolution.

Think, what you are ready to be right now when you *are* ready to be evolution. What would be the beingness right now? If your larger game is *Homo amor*, in Unique Self Symphony, that is beautiful. It is uniquely you doing it.

We are ready to be evolution as a community. Do you see what that could possibly be together? This has never happened before in modern times. We are ready to be evolution, together as the church of Evolutionary Love. You or I cannot do this alone.

Are you ready to participate in the evolution of culture and consciousness? Let's look at that clearly. The evolution of culture means evolving the surrounding ideas and thoughts and innovations that we consider to be modern culture, where we all live. Think about how much you love, or do not love modern culture. What is not so good about it? Modern culture is not a culture of love. Not to love modern culture means we are not ready to participate in a culture of separation.

We are ready to participate in the evolution of culture toward a culture of co-creation where each person is given the opportunity to give their gift to the whole.

And we are ready to participate in the culture of the evolution of consciousness. What I am ready for is to be aware of that consciousness that says, *I am evolution.* As a member of this culture I commit to evolving my deepest understanding, and also to evolving my activation as member of this culture and this consciousness. All of this is playing the larger game toward a planetary awakening in love, as evolution moves toward its own goal.

Do you see the empowerment that comes when all of these are playing out personally?

Lastly, are you ready to participate in the evolution of love? Yes, I am! Are you?

When you do, it's personal in your own intimate life. To say *Yes!* to the evolution of love is not only in general but as the evolution of love *personally.* It is not so much how you love your mate or your child, but how you love the evolution of love as you give your gift to the whole.

What is the feeling of evolution of love? I go through the whole core of the spiral and I feel the inner impulse of the whole impulse of evolution is God, and **God's love, clearly, is for higher consciousness, more freedom, more order and more loving creativity.**

As I am ready to participate in the evolution of love at the highest, I am ready to join my love with God's love as an aspect of the entire process of creation.

EVOLVING THE *DHARMA* IN UNIQUE SELF SYMPHONY

The first step you need to change the world is to know that you can.

It does not mean—here is a very complicated word in modernity which is: *I have to write a whole original new…whatever.* Well, that is not true, you do not have to.

- Your *being* is original.
- Your *Unique Self* is original.
- Your *presence* is original.
- Your *quality of intimacy* is original.

We want to step into a shared *dharma*: a *dharma* is not something made up. The *dharma* is something that we have spent decades working through, and then we articulate a shared *dharma*.

A shared Dharma is a shared language, it is a shared framework for humanity.

What we're doing is articulating the best available shared story, the best shared framework for humanity, at this moment in history. The idea is not, *let me just write a new story*, no, no, no. Let's *create* this one. When I read earlier today this line from an Outrageous Love Letter I received, it was about a *dharma* we said many times: You are *Homo amor*! I am the CosmoErotic Universe in person. I have cosmic significance. But when I hear that reflected back the same *dharma* but in new words that go through someone's unique quality of being, then that actually adds a letter to the Torah.

That is not, *write a new Dharma*. We have this narcissistic idea of originality. No, my originality is my being; it's my quality of beingness.

We cannot create a Unique Self Symphony by everyone playing a different score, no! We create a Unique Self Symphony by everybody playing *the same score but doing jazz within the score*. That is what a Unique Self Symphony is. We have to get that, otherwise it doesn't work.

The second principle is, resonate. *Resonate!* It is not quite that we are *co-creating* a Unique Self Symphony—it's not exactly that. It's like we have written a score of the Symphony, and now **we're deepening the Symphony,**

deepening the music as we co-create—not the score of the Symphony, but the quality and tenor of how the music is played. That difference is enormous! We are not rewriting the score of the Symphony.

Why are yoga studios succeeding around the world—the first new thing post-churches that are succeeding? Because everyone is practicing within some shared framework of yoga and then there is some jazz within yoga. Within the lineage I grew up in, there is enormous creativity and enormous innovation, and everyone is reading the same text. Then, reading that shared text, something deeper emerges. That is how we evolve consciousness. When we open up the space between us, the evolution of love actually happens, ontologically, *for realsies*.

Let's say we have an open moment. I was talking the other day with someone, and we had this moment of clarity, and from that moment of clarity—just a flash of clarity—I wrote the code. In one split second, thirty seconds, the entire code came out perfect. Why? Because there was a moment of clarity, there was a moment of love, there was a moment of Evolutionary Love, there was a moment of Outrageous Love, there was a moment of egoless-ness.

This is what Unique Self is. Unique Self is individuation beyond ego.

Unique Self is the higher individuation of self and creativity and consciousness beyond ego.

It is like everyone sexes but no one sex is the same as any other.

Let's say a phenomenology about sexuality is not about sexuality, but it is about sex, which *models* Eros.

- It is about creativity.
- It is about consciousness.

- ◆ It is about my unique creativity.
- ◆ It is about my unique consciousness.
- ◆ It is about how I do it uniquely.

When I read a line in the beginning from a person who I have been writing these awesome letters together with, and all of a sudden, I hear back and feel, *Oh, wow! They got it!* And they got it in their unique way, they got through their unique quality of being. I read: *We are not trivial!* And when this person writes that, something happens. *We have to take seriously our cosmic significance!* Reading that blows my heart open.

Then when I have another conversation, that blows another part open. We keep blowing each other open. That is what happens. There is a Unique Self Symphony. There is a joining of genius. We are in the *dharma* together.

We have different jobs in the *dharma*. **We have different vocations. We are not supposed to do the same thing.** One problem of the Human Potential Movement is that no one was ever willing to actually surrender. Let's surrender our ego power into Unique Self Symphony power. Let's be together in the *dharma*. Let's each express the *dharma* uniquely.

If anyone has a genuine challenge to the *dharma* because you think we got this wrong, well, bring it on! But do not tell us we got it wrong because *you feel* we are wrong. We will not even listen for a second to that. Tell us that it is wrong because of this reason, with substantive, clear, interior evidence, textual evidence—and then we will evolve the *dharma* with delight! But you do not get to evolve the *dharma* just because you *say* so.

> *You evolve the dharma because you give your entire life to it.*

The same with physics. Can you imagine that you are in Albert Einstein's class and you raise your hand and you say, *relativity? I understand that e*

$= mc^2$ *but I do not really feel it that way.* Really? Are you for real? Did you really just say that?

So, you want to study physics? You want to join the articulation of the *dharma*? Join!

- But give it a couple decades, read day and night, integrate, practice.
- Step in, it is open!
- Meditate! But you can't go into meditation and say, *Oh I meditated, I disagree with Patanjali's meditative instructions because I just do.* Well, no!
- Become a master! There are lots of ways to become a master: come in, study, do Holy of Holies, take our new courses when we offer them, go on the website, just step up, read the books.
- Read *Evolutionary New Testament but* read it twice.
- Read *Unique Self* twice, three times, four times, five times and *then* comment from the inside.
- Practice. Practice. Practice.

Then I am your student. I am your student, but *for realsies.* **That is how you participate in the evolution of love. It is not just a declaration. You can't declare.** You can't be a pioneering soul by just declaring something. That is a first step, but that is not a pioneering. Pioneering means you step in and say, Oh my God, I am going to be a dreamer. And I am going to dedicate and commit wildly and beautifully to go all the way.

So, here is the question you are always asking. You are asking yourself one question: *How deep is your love?* How do you know? Yes, you can spontaneously know as you connect, that is absolutely true, but study is not old paradigm. Study of physics is not old paradigm. The study of *dharma* is not old paradigm. There is no bypassing efforting. Effort and spontaneous go together, If I effort, I have spontaneous awakening. They always move together.

The question we ask ourselves is, with so much humility, with so much divine pride is:

How deep is our love? That is the only question.

How deep is our love? Am I willing to play a larger game? Am I willing to participate in the evolution of love? And I want to give you a promise on the behalf of She: you, me, every single person—we can do this!

We can *actually be* the new story.

We can be the ones we have been waiting for.

We can evolve the source code of culture and consciousness, for real.

Let's go inside and let's blow it open.

CHAPTER SEVEN

EVOLUTION OF LOVE THROUGH PRAYER, ALLUREMENT, AND UNIQUE RISK

Episode 118 — January 12, 2019

EVOLUTIONARY LOVE CODE: AWAKENING AS CONSCIOUS EVOLUTION

This is a code for all of life. Truly. We will read it first here as resonant code and later we will place it into the larger story.

Are you ready to play a larger game?

Are you ready to be evolution?

Are you ready to participate in the evolution of culture and consciousness?

Are you ready to participate in the evolution of love?

Are you ready to love deeper and wider than you ever have before?

Are you ready to include something or someone in your circle of love that has always been on the outside?

Are you ready to change, grow and transform in a way that you have long ago given up on?

Are you ready to be and become more than you ever thought possible?

Are you ready to be a dreamer?

Are you ready to activate Evolutionary Love, in you, as you and through you?

Are you ready to awaken as Conscious Evolution?

EVOLUTION OF LOVE THROUGH PRAYER AND ACTION

Prophecy and prayer are intimate conversations with the Divine.

What does it mean to pray? We want to evolve prayer because evolving prayer is part of participating in the evolution of love. **To evolve prayer means to reclaim an intimate conversation that has been lost in the world. It is the conversation between the human being and God.** There are two great conversations: prayer and prophecy.

- In prayer, the human being initiates and invokes the conversation.
- In prophecy, the Divine initiates and invokes the conversation.
- Both are intimate conversations.

Human creativity often has a dimension of prophecy. There is a moment, a spark of creativity, that moves through us, clearly not of us, and we realize that creativity is an infusion of the Goddess—a divine intoxication. It is a wisdom more wise than we could be, a Spirit more potent than anything we can imagine in our skin-encapsulated ego. The word prophet[9] means

---

9   The word *prophet* in Hebrew, *nabi*, means *speaker*.

speech. It is when I speak more beautifully than I could ever imagine speaking, when that voice moves through me.

And prayer is when I *turn* to the larger field. Prayer is when we say it is not enough for us to be in our skin-encapsulated egos, and we turn to the larger field and invite—plaintively, desperately sometimes—and ask, audaciously demand, intimately beseech the larger field—the Deeper Order, *Ma'at, Geist, Brahmin, Tao, Adonai Elohim*—however we tell the story, that is what we mean by God.

There are two responses in the world to Reality. When Schelling[10] and Leibniz[11] asked, **Why is there something, rather than nothing?** There were two responses to that question.

One is *Oops! Oops! Oops!* We dress up *Oops* in all sorts of ways. We give it all sorts of logical positivism and scientific materialism. We have all sorts of very fancy names. The names for *Oops!* are legion. But basically *Oops!* means, *don't ask!* That is what it means. If you ask, then there is something wrong with you, you haven't grown up, you haven't matured. It is somehow infantile. That is the *Oops!* answer. But, actually, the *Oops!* answer is the most infantile possible answer to the question of: *Why is there something rather than nothing?*

The other answer is some version of: *There is a deeper order.* It has many different names:

- There is a *telos*.
- There is a pattern.
- There is an Intelligence.
- There is *Brahman*.
- There is *Atman* is *Brahman*.
- There is *Adonai hu haElohim*.

---

10   Friedrich Wilhelm Joseph Schelling, a German philosopher
11   Gottfried Wilhelm Leibniz, a prominent German philosopher

There's an Implicate Order, however you tell the story. There's a deeper pattern, this Deeper Order that we sense in Cosmos.

So, in prayer, we move from *Oops!* to the Deeper Order. We turn to the Deeper Order, and we recognize that the Deeper Order is not just a logical order—it is not just an inherent, logical order. It's an Intimate Order. The Infinity that expresses itself, that manifests as a Deeper Order, that we sense in every moment, is intimate, and needs us, loves us, and invites us to love it open with Him/Her/It. It is *Ma'at* and *Geist*, together.[12] Let's feel this together.

Our code today is: Are you ready to participate in the evolution of love?

It means, that *deeper order* turns to us and says,

I cannot do it without you! I love you so much that I manifested a Reality. I turned to you, in relationship, so that you and I, together, could love Reality open. I cannot do it without you!

That is prophecy! That is why God turns to human beings.

Prayer is when we turn to the Deeper Order, and we say: *I cannot do it without You.* I cannot meet my life without You. I want to be in partnership with You and I need Your help. I need Your help to help me fill all of the basic needs I have—my need for stability, my need for prosperity, my need for creativity, and all of those needs You have intimately infused me with. So, we turn to You, Infinity of Intimacy, and we say, *I need You. I need You. I need You.*

If we cannot participate in the evolution of love, our lives feel empty and desiccated and ultimately without a larger flavor of delight.

12 *Ma'at* is an ancient Egyptian concept that represents truth, balance, order, harmony, law, morality, and justice. *Geist* is a German word often translated as *spirit* or *mind*.

The reason my life feels that way, the reason I feel that I need You, is because that is how You have manifested me. So, when we turn to God in prayer, it is really that the God in me turns to the God beyond, and says, *I need you.*

In prophecy, God turns to me. God says, *I—the large, the ultimate, deeper-order God—turn to you, the God in you, and say, Oh my God! We need each other, we need each other.*

When we pray, when we participate in prayer, we turn to the Ultimate and we say:

I need you. I need you. I am going to ask you for everything, and my need is dignified, and you know that because you manifested that need in me, so please, please, please hear me. I know you want to hear me. I love you madly and I need you absolutely and desperately.

Let me bring before you my holy and my broken Hallelujah and offer it, and put it all before you, as lovers do, as Outrageous Lovers do, and I know that:

> You're going to hold every word.
> You're going to kiss every word, and
> You're going to answer every prayer

Sometimes with a yes, and sometimes with a maybe and sometimes with a no. But You are going to hear every word, and You are going to be there in the ultimate response.

As we prepare to participate in the evolution of love we are going to tell the story, a new story as our contribution, the biggest contribution ever. But we cannot do anything unless we first pray. So we come before God, and we come into *Hallelujah,* and we offer it all up.

We offer it all up, everything, the holy and the broken *Hallelujah,* the drunken intoxication, the pristine praise. Prayer affirms the dignity of personal need. **Prayer and prophecy, two sides of that same intimate conversation.** And we ask for everything. We ask directly.

When you pray, something happens neuro-scientifically. We are here—the Church of Evolutionary Love. We are da Vinci. We are in Bethlehem. We are standing for the new order, the new elegant order and for the new story. And we are going to weave all of these prayers together into the story. And in this moment, right now, we are going to cross over to the other side and make the story real in ourselves.

ARE YOU READY TO PLAY A LARGER GAME?

Today's code is an expression of a cosmic love story:

- Are you ready to play a larger game?
- Are you ready to be evolution?
- Are you ready to participate in the evolution of culture?

The evolutionary impulse running through billions of years of evolution is *God in action*. If you really love God you are going to feel, ever more deeply, God in action as you. When God is in action as you, realize what that actually means: **God in action is you and me, right now**. This is a God that took us from nothing at all to Everything-That-Is, the awesomeness and genius of God.

If you have an evolutionary perspective and you are seeing that nothing *just* happens, you are discovering the genius of God. When we say *Yes* and ask, *are you ready to play a larger game?* Who are we asking? What larger game are you getting ready to play if what you are calling is the God in you, unfolding as you?

The God in you is always a threshold in the sense that evolution itself, if you look at it from a truly God perspective—from an external gestalt[13]— you will see this incredible process of evolution, from billions and billions of years. This is the threshold you and I are at right now, at the threshold of

---

13 Gestalt is a German word that means "shape" or "form." In the context of psychology, Gestalt refers to a theory that proposes that the human mind perceives objects as whole rather than as a sum of individual parts. Gestalt can also refer to a holistic approach to understanding phenomena.

that unfolding. The great thing about this community is that it is unfolding, consciously, through us, collectively, as the evolution of love.

Put all that together, and you can see that God is really pleased. In fact, you could say that God has been waiting for this for a long time! The Universe itself is a love story, from quarks to us. What is the nature of that love story? It is totally reinforcing of everything we are doing in this community, for all the five mass extinctions, for all the things that did not work.

The purpose of this Evolutionary Love Story is always going towards three things (and this is, from our great friend Teilhard de Chardin[14]):

- ◆ It's going toward higher consciousness from single cells to us.
- ◆ It's going towards greater love and complexity.
- ◆ It's going toward greater freedom of choice.

It's the value system that God placed in the core of evolution that is in every one of us. And it's in you and me exactly where we are. Internalize it as God's code. God's code is playing a larger game. It's my consciousness in this moment that is the consciousness of the Universe evolving. When we say *Yes,* we're saying *Yes* to that. It's an awesome power. It is not just my personal consciousness.

When we say *Yes,* the second great thing that nature has been working on for billions of years (from quarks to us, from rocks to the internet) is freedom. Ask yourself what the greatest freedom is that this love code of evolution *is offering to you.* You probably have many different choices in your life. You could do this—you could do that. Out of whatever freedom you have, you move toward a greater consciousness of the source of evolution, and toward greater love through greater complexity. This is to say you add more love to your life by *including more people* and reaching out to those outside your current circle.

---

14 Teilhard de Chardin (1881–1955) was a French Jesuit priest, philosopher, and paleontologist known for his ideas on the integration of science and religion. He developed the concept of the Omega Point, a future state of maximum complexity and consciousness towards which he believed the Universe is evolving.

When I say *Yes* to myself, I am saying *Yes* to consciousness, freedom, and more complexity.

An expression of that itself is praying! So, who is praying to whom here? And who is asking? *I am! You are!* Who are we asking? The Thing Itself. Isn't that interesting? The Thing Itself is asking the Thing Itself!

Ask yourself, how do we fit into building a multi-billion-year story of evolution? How come a community of Evolutionary Love has just cropped up? I know of no other community of Evolutionary Love. Many churches are speaking for love and certainly the earliest church of Jesus was *Love me as I have loved you*. Jesus was the personification of the loving human form and that formed the original church. But then so many other things came into those churches.

The development of this community in some respect has a new kind of significance like the very first churches did. People died for those. People lived for those. It totally transformed culture until it got taken over politically. But we are not aiming for taking over politically. **We totally transform culture by doing exactly what we say we were going to do**.

We see our community on planet Earth in different parts of the world at the very moment of quantum breakdown or quantum breakthrough being the protective mothering/fathering love that's going to carry us through the quantum shift.

At this time of the quantum shift on planet Earth, what would you like to contribute to make this community play its role:

- For you?
- For us?
- For society as a whole?

What do you want to give to make this happen? What are you capable of sharing with others? The early churches were formed by people inviting themselves into small communion groups, sharing holy communion together. We commune together, and we find each other.

Take time to make your contribution. Your contribution is utterly essential! Every contribution, every small contribution, helps us to leap forward.

The holiest day of the year, I used to say, is not a day on the calendar. It is not Ramadan (which is a particular holy day in the Middle Eastern countries). It is not Yom Kippur, another holy day.

The holiest day of the year is when the legislature passes the budget, and they decide where they are going to invest resources. Because that is the story.

If I spend more money a month seeing movies than I do in this community, then I can say whatever I want, like: *I'm all for love and light, and I want prosperity*, but I'm basically lying. I'm not telling the truth. If I spend more money on irrelevant things in my life, like having three cable channels and not have 50 USD for Evolutionary Church, I'm a liar. It's okay, but just know that.

I will tell you something very beautiful.

It is only what we do with our money that reveals what our true yearning is.

The Hebrew word *kesef* means money, and *kesefim* means monies, which is a word in the book of Psalms. *Nechsefa nafshi* is a Hebrew phrase in Psalm 84:3, which means yearning and longing. So, the word money can mean yearning and longing. **Money reveals what I yearn for.**

What do I yearn for? It's a very big deal because that is how we build the community. It's the idea Bernie Sanders had when he asked people all across the country to make small contributions that funded his campaign.[15] We are doing a campaign here. This is a campaign for a politics of Evolutionary Love. And everyone knows that a campaign is only successful if it can do its fundraising effectively. No campaign makes it without that.

There's a series of books written about how things rose and fell in Israel with a very famous woman prime minister that some of you may remember, Golda Meir. Golda actually transformed Israel because just before the establishment of Israel, Israel was going bankrupt, and Golda Meir from Wisconsin[16] came to America in 1947 and did an incredibly successful contribution campaign, which saved the state of Israel—there would not have been a state of Israel without it.

So, it's about the ability to locate our yearning, and we locate our yearning through where we resource our lives. And so, I am just giving a huge invitation to everyone to really open your heart and resources.

TAKE YOUR UNIQUE RISK TO CLAIM YOUR ALLUREMENT

How do we participate in the evolution of love? Let's make this super-practical. What are we drawn to in the world? We have an idea we talked about, which is allurement. Allurement is one of the qualities of love. It is one of the qualities of Eros. Allurement means we are drawn to something; we are moved towards it. It is Unique Self, which is the core part of the new story.

---

15 Bernie Sanders' 2016 and 2020 campaigns used the rhetoric: We don't represent the interests of billionaires. We don't want their money. We don't need their money. This campaign is about the needs of working people and the poor, and we are proving that we can run a winning campaign powered by small contributions from millions of Americans.

16 Golda Meir, the fourth Prime Minister of Israel, spent part of her early life in Wisconsin. Although she was born in Kyiv, Ukraine, in 1898, her family emigrated to the United States in 1906 to escape anti-Semitic violence in Eastern Europe. They initially settled in Milwaukee, Wisconsin, where Meir grew up and attended school.

To be *Homo amor* means we are a unique set of allurements. We are uniquely allured.

That is the structure of reality, just like protons, electrons, neutrons, and atoms. Atoms are uniquely allured to each other. There is a unique structure of allurement and only particular atoms can come together and make a particular new relationship. To know our allurement, we have to get clear. We go inside and we clarify our allurement.

Allurement is one of the qualities of Eros. Eros has many qualities.

The first step is the clarification of allurement, as Isaac Luria, one of my lineage teachers called *berur*. *Berur* means the clarification of desire and allurement. What do we desire? What do we *really desire*? It's what Buddha was talking about in the original Pali Canon[17] when he said, *have few desires but have great ones*. What are we really allured to?

Our unique allurement is what we are most drawn to, what we are most *allured* to do, within the context of our lives. There are all sorts of pseudo allurements. There are pseudo desires. You can do everything in the world on two levels. You can do things to get a hit of dopamine: We can do writing to get dopamine hits. We can do sexing to get dopamine hits. We can start Evolutionary Churches to get dopamine hits.

We feel empty, we want to cover the emptiness—so we do some exterior activity to get dopamine, that is pseudo allurement. That is pseudo-eros. Because we feel empty, we usually look unconsciously to cover the emptiness, and we cover the emptiness with a kind of pseudo allurement and pseudo-eros. But ultimately, it does not work. The emptiness stays empty.

We have to find our great desires. When Buddha says, *have few desires but have great ones,* what Buddha misses—with all due respect—is the

---

17   The Pali Canon, also known as the Tipitaka, is a vast collection of scriptures in the Theravada Buddhist tradition. When referencing the Pali Canon, it is essential to be specific about the particular book, sutta, and even the section or verse number.

uniqueness. It is not just, *have few desires but have great ones*, but: **Your great desire is the desire that is unique to you. It is your unique set of allurements.**

Step 2 is to claim my unique allurement. First, we are willing to clarify, then we are willing to claim. I have to claim my unique allurement. Claim! It is yours! It is waiting to be claimed by you.

> This is what I *madly love* to do.
> This is what I am *drawn* to do.

I am willing to claim my unique allurement. I'm willing to claim it. I have to claim it. Once I claim my allurement, I have to go the next step, **step three**. Step three is critical! My unique allurement is what I am most drawn to, what I am most allured to within the context of my life. So, if I would say I'm most drawn to run for president in 2020, the truth is, I am! I'd like to run for president, but right now I have to finish a bunch of great, critical books, "Homo amor" etcetera, so I'm not going to run for president in 2020. I might in 2024. I am not taking that off the table. Maybe we have the Evolutionary Church run for president together. I'm not taking that off the table, but my allurement has to work in the context of my life.

First, I have to claim my allurement. I have to claim it: *This is my allurement.*

And then: let myself want. Let the experience of want and desire rise in me.

We have taken desire off the table. We have talked about a God without needs and desire. That is a huge mistake. Every stream of religion has at some point made this mistake and said, *God is beyond needs and desires.* That is not true! That is *one taste of Divinity*—the taste of perfection.

But there is a *second taste of Divinity,* which is the desire of the Infinite, the allurement.

Infinity is allured to the finite.

That's what Blake meant when he said, *Infinity loves the productions of time.*[18] Infinity is allured, drawn to the finite. Then Divinity, God, Infinity, claims that allurement and takes a third step: **I am willing to take my unique risk in order to claim my allurement.**

You cannot do it without a unique risk. There is always a unique risk. So, step three is: *I am willing to take my unique risk.*

My unique risk might be, Oh my God, *I am going to take six months off—let me take a huge unique risk to make a gorgeous contribution.* That is a big risk; it is a big deal; it is huge. We want to recognize and honor that and be delighted. I am willing to take my unique risk in order to claim my allurement.

Now a risk is not reckless. A risk is the road. When it is my unique risk, my risk is the road to rapture. My unique risk is the road to rapture. Really get this: I'm willing to take my unique risk in order to claim my allurement, and my unique risk is not reckless. It is huge to understand. It is not irresponsible. My unique risk is not reckless at all! It's not about being irresponsible.

My unique risk is the road to responsibility and rapture.

That is wild! There is no split between responsibility and rapture. Responsibility and rapture, R&R. That is the new form of R&R. My unique risk is the road to responsibility and rapture. Let's get excited about this!

It is ontological, meaning my unique risk is the road to responsibility and rapture for *realsies*!

---

18   *The Marriage of Heaven and Hell* (1790-1793). This work is one of Blake's most famous and serves as a complex, visionary text that explores the nature of opposites, such as good and evil, heaven and hell, and eternity and time.

My rapture is giving my unique gift for the sake of the evolution of love. It is rapturous. It is ecstatic! My rapture is giving my unique gift for the sake of the evolution of love. That is true.

And we are writing this code; we're impressing this code on the lips of the source code. We are impressing this code on the lips of God. We're actually participating together right now in articulating these steps—we're literally participating in the evolution of love. We have never articulated these steps before like this. It's emerging from our being together. We are doing it in the space in between, it's the holy space between all of us.

And there's only one question we need to ask in order to do this together, and it's wild.

One question only: *How deep is our love?*

CHAPTER EIGHT

UNIQUE SELF AS THE WILLINGNESS TO DREAM AGAIN

Episode 119 — January 19, 2019

DARE TO DREAM AGAIN

We are focusing on one part of the code from last time (see episode 118) : *Are you ready to be a dreamer?* Let's dream vividly.

Martin Luther King said, *I have a dream,* and we want to give our *We Have a Dream* speech.

We are going from, *I have a dream,* to *We have a dream,* to dreaming 3.0! It is the next step.

- Dreaming 1.0: when dreams were all about portents from the gods—which is beautiful.
- Dreaming 2.0: dreams became the topic of Jung's Red Book.[19] Psychoanalysis says, let's work out what is going on in the unconscious.

---

19   C.G. Jung, *The Red Book: Liber Novus,* ed. Sonu Shamdasani, trans. Mark Kyburz, John Peck, and Sonu Shamdasani (New York: Norton, 2009).

- Dreaming 3.0: We dream as God. Evolution dreams as us. Does everyone get that?

This is Dreaming 3.0! We are evolution's dream awakening through us! In Dreaming 3.0 is not: *I have a dream*. It is: *We have a dream*.

So, let's find our dreams! *We have a dream!* We are going to write the *We have a dream* speech and impress it on the lips of Divinity. Let's reach deep because, as we all know, we have forgotten dreams. We forget dreams so easily. We had dreams when we were young and then, somehow, the dreams went away. Somehow, we stopped dreaming.

Remember Harry Chapin[20] and the song "Cat's in the Cradle"? He had another song called "W.O.L.D."[21] about forgetting your dreams. We forget our dreams—so we are here to recapture our dreams. Not just the personal dream, but the *We Have a Dream*. But *We Have a Dream* doesn't work unless *I* have a dream.

To participate in what we call the Unique Self Jazz Symphony I have to bring my dream to the Symphony. I cannot just play the old score. I have to dream a new dream.

Hafiz[22] suggests: *Row, row, row, our boat gently down the stream for the ocean refuses no river that remembers to dream.* Because dreams are made up of all of the sweetness and all of the shattering, of all of the rough and all of the rapture.

---

20   Chapin, H., & Chapin, S. (1974). "Cat's in the Cradle," *Verities & Balderdash*. Elektra Records

21   W.O.L.D. by Harry Chapin: https://www.youtube.com/watch?v=QVh6aOwY08g

22   The famous Persian poet, Meher Baba, expresses the idea of spiritual unity and the eventual return of all souls to God, much like rivers flowing back into the ocean, with the central teachings about love, acceptance, and the divine journey of the soul. Hafiz explores themes of love, joy, and the divine, encouraging a lighthearted and playful approach to existence: *Just sit there right now. Don't do a thing. Just rest. For your separation from God is the hardest work in this world.* Daniel Ladinsky, *The Gift: Poems by Hafiz, the Great Sufi Master* (Penguin Compass, 1999).

Our deepest unique risk is to dream again, and to let God/Goddess love me open into dreams again, and to know that even when dreams shatter, we can dream them again, more deeply.

- ◆ We need our dreams.
- ◆ We need to be dreamers.
- ◆ We need to live in a country, and in a world which supports dreams.

So, when we turn to God in prayer, and ask for everything, every personal need that we have, we affirm the dignity of our personal need. If we don't affirm the dignity of personal need, we can't dream. My unique risk is to dare to dream. **My deeper unique risk is to dare to dream *again*, after my dreams were shattered a thousand times and I was betrayed a million times.**

You know what, world? We are going to dream again!

Oh my God! I am not going to dream by myself. We are going to be together here in the Church of Evolutionary Love. We have to dream together. We cannot dream alone. No person, no human being, can dream alone. *Lo-tov heyot ha'adam levado.*[23] It says in the Bible, it is not good for the human being to be lonely. We are rewriting the new sacred scripture. **It's not good for the human being to dream alone.**

Our dreams are the most intimate. We are going to dream together. Dreamers we are.

GOD'S DREAM: THE EVOLUTION OF CONSCIOUSNESS AND FREEDOM

Are you ready to be a dreamer?

Imagine that out of no-thing at all came a dream, and God's dream was invisible. There was no visibility. There was nothing.

---

23   Genesis 2:18

But out of that incredible impulse, which was by far the most brilliant, intelligent thing that can be imagined—out of no-thing at all came the first glimmers of connectivity, of different elements coming together for billions and billions of years. God's dream is always for more consciousness, to go from things that had no consciousness at all, from single cells to multi-cells, to the animals, to humans to Evolutionary Love.

Let's take God's dream into our own consciousness and dream at the same level of consciousness that would be equal to the impulse of creation itself that created all this. Let's take our *ready to be a dreamer* right at the edge of our own consciousness and dream it into its next extraordinary experiential reality.

Then, let's notice what God's dream has been while organizing this most massively intelligent Universe. He/She is putting more and more freedom into every stage of the dream, just as the multi-cell is far more free than the single cell—all the way on up to *Homo sapiens sapiens*—far freer than an animal—and now to us: *Homo evolutionary, Homo conscious evolutionary*.

We have been given the freedom that no other species has ever achieved on this Earth: to destroy all of life, Boom! Or to evolve all of life. We have been given freedom to do that and have our own unique desire to dream our own potential into the system.

Let's include our own dreaming, our freedom, and our wholeness. Let's dream the whole way.

Finally, if we are ready to be a dreamer, we are dreaming our consciousness forward, we are dreaming our freedom to be greater. Let's dream our connectivity and love—the complexity that we are bringing together—where everyone is a dreamer, connecting in their dreams for the fulfillment of the individual, the society, and the world.

God is dreaming with us when we are dreaming God's dream.

We are dreaming of:

- Greater consciousness
- Greater freedom
- Greater loving order for every one of us

We are dreaming for the evolution of Conscious Evolution. That means our dreams have become consciously created as us; that God is giving us the power for Conscious Evolution, for our dreams.

Let's take a moment together to dream of Evolutionary Love, for greater consciousness of that love, for greater freedom and for more complex connectivity around the world.

Can you hold that with us, together, to dream the dream of Evolutionary Love together? Does anyone have a collective dream and is dreaming to use the Evolutionary Church as a vehicle to manifest this dream? We are dreaming the dream of Evolutionary Love from the perspective of conscious evolution, of existence itself, from the origin of creation to the present. We are dreaming this dream!

Ervin Laszlo, in *Science and the Akashic Field*[24] points out that every one of us is a million, billion cells—more than the number of stars in the Milky Way—over 600 billion cells in every one of us dying right now, and the same number regenerating, right now! There is primacy of the inseparable whole. We could not possibly be doing this as little individual cells.

Let's place our dreaming as God would dream it, with our trillions of cells together, dreaming, as a vibrational, awesome intelligence as the Universe itself, dreaming. Are we ready to dream together? Are we ready to activate our individual dream and say internally *yes* and let that dream be activated as clearly as possible? Are we ready to activate the dreamer as part of a collective—for everyone to be able to dream the largest contribution they could possibly make, to evolve as a dreamer—and **go one step further than we've ever gone before: dreaming love for humanity and for everyone in it?**

---

24   Ervin Laszlo, *Science and the Akashic Field: An Integral Theory of Everything* (Inner Traditions, 2004).

DREAMING OF WHOLE MATES

To really love each other is to truly dream together.

At that particular moment, when we can see the dream together, the difference between a soul mate and a whole mate is that soul mates dream a small dream, role mates dream of family—nuclear family. Let's build our family, *our* nuclear family which is unbelievably beautiful.

My brother's wife made a bar *mitzvah* for their 13-year-old. They were dancing, and they were joyous, and it was gorgeous. At the same time, I realized that this is an egocentric, ethnocentric dream. This is blood relations, so it is egocentric—my survival clan. We are part of the same ethnocentric community.

As I was listening and looking at these pictures I said, *What are we trying to do here in Evolutionary Church*? We want to be a band of Outrageous Lovers who are dreaming together, beyond blood relations, beyond an ethnocentric community. **We are dreaming together because what unites us is the dream.**

- The dream is not limited by an ethnocentric predicament.
- It is not limited by religion.
- It is not limited by a border.

It is a dream of no-boundary consciousness. It is a dream that says that we look at the horizon, together.

Soul mates and role mates dream about their ego and ethnocentric world.

But soul mates dream particularly, very beautifully, about the beauty of their love for each other. It is *Love Story*, 1970! That is when it started coming into culture. As Paul McCartney sang, *I can't believe there's another silly love song!*[25]

---

25   Paul McCartney, "Silly Love Songs." *Wings at the Speed of Sound*, Capitol Records, 1970.

All love songs are gorgeous and they are almost always about soul mates. It is about our particular dream. But to move to whole mate is to dream the bigger dream.

Are you willing to dream a bigger dream? Are we willing to *dream a whole mate* dream?

- Whole mates look at the horizon together.
- Whole mates share a dream. That is what binds them at the core.
- Whole mates are dreamers together.

Sometimes whole mates are revealed and sometimes they are hidden, but they are dreaming together, and it is that dream. They may have a role mate dimension, they may have a soul mate dimension, but:

At their core whole mates are united by the strange attractor of a dream beyond imagination.

It is a dream of a world that works for everyone. It is a dream of the word DACA,[26] where children of immigrants who came to the country have a path to citizenship so they can create this great country together with us. We are at a moment where people are having less sex, and our birth rate numbers are going down. There is an enormous amount of literature on that in this last year. We are going in the same direction Japan did, which means that:

- Our financial base is shrinking.
- Our base of creative intelligence is shrinking.
- The way we have to augment and reinvigorate that in

---

26 Deferred Action for Childhood Arrivals (DACA) is an immigration policy implemented by the United States Department of Homeland Security (DHS).

the American context is by actually having an intelligent immigration.

That is true in every context. An intelligent policy of immigration—which is a huge and complex issue, and one pillar of that issue is DACA—must include dreams. Children of illegal immigrants can have a way to citizenship and to contribute to this great dream.

We need to find a way to create a way for populations to exchange while retaining the integrity of the Unique Self of each culture. That is one of the great challenges in the world today. We need a language to have conversations with. That is what the *dharma* is: it is a language to have every conversation.

Our question today is: Are we willing to dream a bigger dream?

As a separate self I dream about me and my survival people. That is my dream, and it is a beautiful dream. As separate selves we become role mates in relationship when we dream about the family. That is an egocentric dream, and the ego is beautiful! That is not a negative ego, this is a positive, healthy ego-strength. The ability to dream, as a separate self, is the mark of a healthy personality, of a healthy person—that's gorgeous! We cannot skip our personal dreams. It is why we do not skip asking for our personal needs in prayer. We can never skip personal dreams.

- I am going to live in the right place.
- I want to not be lonely on my walks in the afternoon.
- I want to feel met by my neighbors.
- I want to have enough prosperity to buy even an old, ramshackle house and put it together exactly the way I want it.

Never skip personal desire. My personal desire affirms the dignity of my separate-self personhood. That is the beginning, that is what psychology taught us. That is the beginning of being in integrity with myself.

But then we want to dream more. But before we get to dream more, we go from separate self to my false self and my dream often distorts. My false self desperately wants to be seen, which is beautiful, but it gets desperate, it gets twisted, it gets distorted. We make wrong decisions.

Is there somebody who has not made a wrong decision? Or someone whose dream did not get distorted somewhere, did not get confused? Is there someone who did not, at some point, see through what the mystics call in Aramaic *baryara lo awkiya*—an unclear prism? **Everyone, at some point, dreams through an unclear prism.**

The mystics say that when Abraham had a dream and God said, *sacrifice your son,* he was dreaming through an unclear prism. He was dreaming through a cultural prism because his father, Terach, had brought him to be sacrificed to the deity-king Nimrod. So, in a kind of repetition-compulsion, Abraham dreams that same dream. It is repetition-compulsion. His dream is distorted.

Sometimes we dream dreams to please our father and mother, but it is not our dream, so our dreams get distorted. Our false self distorts our dreams. We dream through an unclear prism. We have to clarify our prism. Dreaming is not that easy.

- Dreaming is a high art.
- Dreaming is high dignity.
- Dreaming is divinity.

Divinity dreams. God dreamed and there came the world. Let's feel this together. A world in which every human being is, as we said earlier, 50 trillion cells in gorgeous existential complementarity beyond imagination. That is the divine dream!

THE SHATTERING OF THE VESSELS AND HEALING THROUGH DREAMING DEEPER

In the mystical tradition, Divinity dreams the world several times, and the worlds fell apart. The dreams did not work. There's a great text from the third century which says *borei olamot u'macharivan*[27]—God created, and dreamed worlds, and those worlds got destroyed, until we were able to dream a good dream. So, let's notice, friends, that we have to clarify our dreams. When we move from separate self to false self, our dreams get distorted.

And number two, our dreams shatter.

It is the same mystical tradition that Habermas[28] and Walter Benjamin[29] loved so much and that Gershom Scholem[30] wrote about. If you go to the Guggenheim-Museum in New York, there's a quote from Gershom Scholem, the great Hebrew mystic, which captures what the museum is about.

In Hebrew mysticism there's this notion that the divine dream shatters God, Divinity, Infinity, dreams, and light into vessels—and then those vessels shatter, *shevirat haKelim*:

---

27   Midrash Bereshit Rabbah 3:7

28   Jürgen Habermas is a prominent German philosopher and sociologist known for his work in critical theory, communicative action, and discourse ethics. As part of the Frankfurt School tradition, his theories build on the works of thinkers like Max Horkheimer, Theodor Adorno, and Herbert Marcuse, yet he also critiques and extends their ideas, especially concerning democracy, rationality, and modernity.

29   Walter Benjamin was a German-Jewish philosopher, cultural critic, and literary theorist associated with the Frankfurt School, though his work was more eclectic and less systematically aligned with their critical theory than thinkers like Adorno and Horkheimer. His interests spanned a wide range of topics, from aesthetics and literature to history, politics, and theology. Benjamin is known for his original and sometimes fragmented style of writing, combining Marxist ideas with Jewish mysticism and surrealism.

30   Gershom Scholem (1897–1982) was a German-born Israeli philosopher and historian, widely regarded as the founder of the modern academic study of *Kabbalah*, the Jewish mystical tradition.

The shattering of the vessels is the shattering of the dreams.

If you want to know what the shattering of the vessels is in your life, find the moment when your dreams shattered.

Let's do something a little bit hard. Just say, *I am willing to find the moment when my dreams shattered.* We cannot skip this step. We all have moments like that. I know that moment. I can find four moments when my dreams shattered. We cannot cover that up. I have to be willing to find the moment when it broke, where the vessels broke. I am willing to find the moment when my dreams shattered!

 If we skip this step, we cannot get there. We cannot do a bypass. There is no evolutionary bypass, there is no New Age bypass, there is no human potential bypass. There is no fundamentalist religion bypass.

I have to be willing to find the moment when my dreams shattered. That is the broken *Hallelujah*.

- It might have been a separate self-moment.
- It might have been a false self-moment.
- It might have been a moment of betrayal—we have all been betrayed and we have all, on some level, also betrayed.

We are not innocent. We want to find our second innocence, our innocence beyond. You can only be betrayed by someone who would never betray you. So, if we find that moment where our dream shattered, it is from that place we move to True Self.

In True Self we are inseparable from the One, and the One lives in me. We are not dreaming anymore a personal dream. In True Self, we let go of the personal dream. *We dream for the world. We dream for everything.* We bypassed ourselves. We are in True Self. The total number of True Selves in the world is one. There is *one* True Self, just one. It is Essence. True Self and

115

Essence are the same thing: *I am one with.* The smallness of the personal falls away, and we dream the large, beautiful dream of open blue sky and vast expanse and gorgeous, spacious, infinite bliss. It is a gorgeous dream for every human being.

But then we dream deeper.

We're willing to dream deeper because we have to find the personal beyond True Self, the personal beyond the impersonal. We have to find the personal face of Essence awake and alive in us. Only personal dreams heal the contraction of the ego. **You can't heal the ego through separate self or True Self. You have to get to Unique Self, which is when we actually reclaim our personal dreams. Unique Self is when we are willing to dream again.**

Let's all go to that place where we found that our dreams shattered and claim the voice of Unique Self which is:

I am willing to dream again.

Yes! We are at that point where our dreams shattered. We are standing at that abyss of darkness and we are *not* a victim. We are a player, and we are going to rewrite this story—not as a victim story, not as a detour, but as a destination.

From that place of broken vessels, we are going to heal the shattered vessels, and we are going to dream again. But this time it is not just: *I have a dream.* It is: *We have a dream.* We are willing to dream again as Unique Self and we know that our dream is unlike any other. Each of our dreams is utterly unique. And yet, when my dream resonates with another, when I find that whole mate or that group of whole mates, when I find that individual whole mate with whom I'm resonating in the same frequency, and then we can look at each other and say, *we can dream together.*

Then we ask, *How deep is my love*? Am I willing to dream again? Am I willing to say, together: *We have a dream?* And are we going to dream it together with a million people?

That becomes a political and social force, a rising tide for healing unlike any other, which is the healing of transformation of All-That-Is.

Let's impress it on our hearts and on God's lips. ***We have a dream!***

CHAPTER NINE

ALLUREMENT TO EVER INCREASING INTIMACY

Episode 120 — January 26, 2019

EVOLUTIONARY LOVE CODE: YOUR UNIQUE RISK

Your unique risk is not reckless. It is a natural expression of your Unique Self.

Your Unique Self is, at one level, your unique set of allurements. Be faithful to the integrity of your original allurement even after it has faded, and it will return.

The only genuine reckless risk that anyone can truly take is a risk that endangers your very life at its most essential root which is to *not* take your unique risk.

Your unique risk will not be self-evidently supported by those closest to you, at least not initially. But eventually, as your authenticity, depth and steadiness deepens over the years, your unique risk will attract new people into your life, evolutionary partners and beloveds with whom you can go the whole way in this lifetime.

Sometimes your partner in marriage or family might be beautiful and perfect but might *not* be the one who can fathom the depth of your unique risk. And that is fine.

119

YOU CAN TRUST YOUR ALLUREMENT

What do you need to take the unique risk? In order to know what your unique risk is, you need two things. One, you need an original allurement. There is an original allurement. That is step one. You have to trust and find what are you drawn to. Your Unique Self *is* your unique set of allurements. You have to trust your allurement:

- When you are allured to a path
- When you are allured to a teacher
- When you are allured to a *dharma*
- When you are allured to a beloved
- When you are allured to a vocation

Trust your allurement, number one. That is step one.

Two: know that your allurement *will always fade*.

It will always happen. It will never not happen. Your allurement will always fade.

It's why Madonna sings, *Like a virgin for the very first time.* What she means is there is an original allurement in the sexual, but the sexual models Eros. All fields of Eros are like that. There's an original allurement, and then that allurement always fades. Always! Never does it not! That is step two—when the allurement fades.

Step three is when you reclaim your allurement, that original allurement. You reclaim it, but not because it is a gift from the heavens.

At level one, it's called *le'huta de-le'ela—arousal from above.* It is a gift. You hear someone's voice, you see someone, you see an idea, you are drawn to a place, you are drawn to a teacher, to a friend, to a beloved, to a path, to a vocation, and you are like, *Oh my God! I am home! I am so allured!*

Allurement drives Cosmos.
Reality is allurement.

There is nothing underneath allurement. Electromagnetic attraction, gravity, it is all allurement. Allurement is primary.

- Step one: I feel my allurement and I follow it. I follow my *clarified* allurement, not my surface allurement.
- Step two: the allurement fades.
- Step three: I open my heart again, but this time it is *le'uta de-letata* in Aramaic—*arousal from below.* I *choose* my allurement.

I am choosing the same allurement that was gifted to me. It is kind of like that analogy: you get a free download—one of these ninety-day free downloads—and then you have to buy the program.

So, I have the allurement: level one; allurement fades: level two; and then I open my heart again and reclaim the allurement: level three. To do that, you have to be always practicing—to be in that meditation of Outrageous Love.

To know my unique risk, I have to be in allurement. You can't know your unique risk outside of the frame of allurement. Your Unique risk makes no sense without allurement.

I need allurement, and I need reclaimed allurement at that place of level three, of reclaiming my allurement. From there my unique risk is clear, and it's usually the same as it was at level one but this time, I am *choosing* it. It's unique risk, but *not by chance.* It's unique risk *by choice.* That's where choice happens. It's a very big deal that I can actually choose it, because when I choose it, the purpose of my life is realized.

To have a unique set of allurements means we are personally addressed by the Infinity of Allurement, by Cosmos itself. When we experience ourselves as being personally addressed, we relax.

Only personal allurement, only the notion, the realization, that Reality is alluring me personally releases the contraction of the pain of our life.

Allurement is not just a gravitational or electromagnetic quality. Allurement personally addresses me. The Infinity of Intimacy turns to me personally and allures me.

Allurement is enchanted attraction.

An enchanted attraction is not when I go blind. My eyes open when I actually experience an enchanted attraction.

- ◆ I do not go blind.
- ◆ I do not lose my autonomy.
- ◆ I do not lose my integrity.
- ◆ I do not lose my rationality.

It is beyond my rationality. It is my deepest identity. I am uniquely allured.

When we know that Reality is turning to me and saying, *I am seducing you*—but not seduction in a narrow sense of *to give up myself*; rather, seduction beyond my narrowness, seduction beyond my contraction, seduction beyond my smallness into the space of my wider self.

When we take the lid off and go all the way, when we sing in the shower, we bring it all before the Divine. To do that you got to always be practicing. We are always in that meditation of Outrageous Love. So, let's love each other madly. We believe in mad love as Rumi calls it.

In a world that is often insane, the only way to be sane is to love madly, to love outrageously, all the way home.

WHEN YOU SAY YES TO ALLUREMENT, IT SAYS YES TO YOU

Allurement is the impulse of evolution. The inner impulse is personalizing in us, powerfully, and often ripping us out of our past. We are awakening as a new species of evolutionaries.

I'll tell you briefly the story of people who transformed me by helping me to recognize my allurement.

As you are thinking about your own allurement, ask yourself, *where does it get turned on? And by whom?*

When I was in Paris in 1948 after the Second World War, I discovered there was almost nothing but depression there. There was no sense of allurement, they didn't believe that you could have faith in anything anymore, because they had been so defeated. Millions of people had been killed, and the Nazis had taken over. There was a social depression that suppressed allurement.

My allurement started with the creation of the atomic bomb. I thought, *we have this power, we have to be alert to the meaning of our power* and I couldn't find anybody who had a clue, including President Eisenhower.

I was having lunch alone one day when a young man walked in and sat opposite me. I asked him my typical question: *What do you think is the meaning of our new power that is good?* He said to me, *I'm an artist, and* **I'm seeking a new image of man commensurate with our power to shape the future.**

The moment I heard this, my inner voice said, *I'm going to marry you.* I got my first definition of allurement right there. I found my deep, passionate power through saying yes to my allurement:

*I am going to be a
shaper of the future.*

So, we got married. I can remember walking down the aisle towards that priest thinking this is wrong. I shouldn't be marrying for my allurement. I want to create a new image of man. Do I want to get married? What does marriage have to do with this?

Well, I got married and I had five children, and each one of those children was an allurement that I experienced with great passion. Then they had to pursue their own allurement. I became a complete support system for my husband and five children. Until one day I heard a voice on the phone. It was Jonas Salk.[31] He called me up and he said, *you have written something. I would like to meet with you. Can I take you to lunch?*

Now, five children, a husband, the house, the gardens, the dogs, the cats, everything to support the allurement of family, and the allurement of girl's purpose.

This allurement was great, but here is what happened. The minute I heard Jonas's voice, I could hardly wait to meet him, and when I did, he said, *this looks to me like the Garden of Eden*—that very beautiful place in the Berkshires. And I answered, *do you know what? I am Eve, and I am leaving.* That was an awesome thing to say about the allurement!

It is not that we don't keep rewarding allurement but, in my case, if I did not keep on moving, I could not keep the past allurements fully alive. Jonas said, *Barbara, you are a mutant!* This is the first time I ever heard of the new human. *You are a mutant, and I am going to introduce you to a few other mutants.* So, I met two or three others: the editor of *Life* magazine; then this one, and that one. Suddenly I was in a totally different domain.

But Jonas Salk was not the man for me. He had his own life, and he was focused on building the Salk Institute. So, here is another thing I learned

---

31   Jonas Salk and Barbara Marx Hubbard's collaboration, while it did not produce any formal collaborative works, books, or papers, was more philosophical and intellectual, focusing on shared themes of human evolution, consciousness, and the ethical implications of scientific advancements. Their ideas mutually influenced each other and the broader movement of Conscious Evolution. Salk's book *Survival of the Wisest* and Hubbard's writings on Conscious Evolution reflect the themes they explored together.

about allurement: I was very allured to him, and I also loved my husband, my dogs, all my children. And here is what happened: I came up with a very interesting way to deal with this, I said: *I have to be able to attract the wild horses of desire*[32] *to something better than longing for Jonas Salk allurements.* I had an image of myself as a charioteer with these horses. These were the wild horses of desire that were leading me astray. So, I asked, *Okay, wild horses, where do I really want to go?* And I will cut a very long story short:

- ◆ I wanted to go into conscious evolution.
- ◆ I wanted to not be supporting somebody else.
- ◆ I wanted to not be allured to somebody else, or somebody else's attractor, or attraction.

What happened then was I got allured by the New Testament. I was allured, seeing all the new technologies I was learning through Jonas. We were going to transform the body. We were going to live much longer lives. We were going to overcome most of the human ailments.

I asked, *Where is my example of this?* In the New Testament Jesus said, *You will do the works that I do, and greater works than these will you do, during the fullness of time.*[33] So, I almost became a member of the Catholic community of Evolutionary Sisters. I loved them and they all loved Teilhard de Chardin.[34] I became a Teilhardian, Catholic, Jesus-inspired Evolutionary.

---

32   The "wild horses of desire" refer to powerful, often uncontrollable impulses or longings that drive a person toward various pursuits or attractions. These desires can be intense and passionate, pulling individuals in different directions, much like wild horses that are difficult to tame. In the context of the narrative, the wild horses of desire symbolize the strong, sometimes chaotic urges that lead the person away from their true path or deeper purpose. By acknowledging and directing these desires, the individual seeks to harness their energy towards a more meaningful and fulfilling goal.

33   See John 14:12.

34   Pierre Teilhard de Chardin (1881–1955) was a French Jesuit priest, scientist, paleontologist, theologian, and philosopher known for his work integrating science and spirituality. His thoughts and writings aimed to reconcile Christian theology with the scientific understanding of evolution and the cosmos.

That only lasted for a time. Then I came back and I tried to think what to do with all of this.

I got a divorce. I had two dozen sincere "conversations" to bring people together. Then John[35] died. And Earl[36] died. I was pretty much left thinking maybe I had done everything.

I did a great big event called Earth 2012, and then I discovered in Marc another mutant whose inner impulse of evolution was allurement, expressed one hundred percent in words, in books, in tapes, and consciously in action.

Suddenly, inner allurement turned on as my own. There was nothing that could turn it off because I had met a person whose allurement related to my own. It is a very deep thing to say. We are joining together now to form the church of Evolutionary Love, as we are joining to write the books that can offer this, as we are reaching out to meet more and more people who are, let's say, new humans building a new humanity based on Evolutionary Love, of which this church is an awesome gathering. I have incarnated the allurement. I discover it is the impulse of evolution itself running through everything and everyone. I have said one hundred percent *Yes* to it, and:

> *When you say Yes to that inner allurement, it says Yes to you!*

So, at the age of ninety I feel new! Because evolution is *always new*. To say wholly *Yes* to allurement, the willingness to take risks for allurement, the fact that it is always right when you are following a deep allurement—even though it has been painful, it has never been wrong. Now as a church, we're going for evolutionary allurement on a planetary scale.

---

35 John Marx, Barbara's brother
36 Barbara Marx Hubbard was married to Earl Hubbard, an artist-philosopher, whom she met in Paris in 1949 and married in 1951.

Our goal is the planetary awakening in love through a Unique Self Symphony which would be *mass allurement,* awakened on a planetary scale, to shift the system from fear to love.

A NEW ALLUREMENT: FROM SELF TO TRIBE, TO WORLD, TO COSMOS

I want to locate ourselves where we are. We are at this place between utopia and dystopia. Let's really get the deep structure. Let's take the next step.

The world operates, and it has for the last several thousand years, on win/lose metrics. In win/lose metrics, you basically have winners and losers. There are people who, for whatever reason are able to take advantage of the system. Sometimes because:

- They are stronger.
- They are more brutal.
- They are clever.
- They inherited money.
- They are more pathological.
- They are is more skillful.

There are a lot of reasons, but it is a win-lose system and the game theoretic of a win-lose system is: there are winners and there are losers. The problem is a win-lose system is a *rivalrous system.*

A rivalrous system means we are not allured to each other. Rivalrous conflict means there is no allurement between us. It works like this: I remove you from play in order to make myself the winner. That is the win-lose system that has dominated the world. It is not just that I *want* something. I want something and I do *not want* you to have it. I want a Rolls Royce, but I do not want you to have one. Because if everybody has a Rolls Royce, well, that is not good! I want to be wealthy, but I do not want everyone to be wealthy because if everyone is wealthy then I think I am not wealthy.

We define ourselves based not on having abundance, but on *having more* than other people. You get that distinction. It is a critical distinction. That's win/lose metrics.

We stand at the risk of biowarfare, with exponential tech, with nanotech, with the merger of biotech and infotech, which births AI—artificial intelligence, with all of its complexities. The new technologies have created the possibility of exponential tech, but exponential tech takes the win-lose system that we have and makes it not just *unsustainable*; it makes it utterly destructive of Reality. Reality cannot stand a world in which exponential tech exponentially increases our power.

So, we can increase our power. We don't just have a fist, we do not just have a spear, we don't just have a tank. We have rogue nuclear weapons owned by non-state actors that are not controlled by a world acting according to the principles of cooperation.

We have a world of non-allurement.

We have what David Snowden called a *complicated* system. We have a complicated system of these different pieces. The pieces in a complicated system operate unaware of and unconcerned with their relationship to the whole—beyond any calculation of wining or losing. These different pieces are at war with each other, just as they've always been. Wars have always sucked; however, you have exponential suck when you have exponential tech—to such a degree that **reality collapses and destroys itself.** That is where we are right now. What do we have to do?

---

*We have to change from
a complicated system to a
complex system.*

What is a complex system?

A complex system is a self-organizing Universe. The body is a complex system. You have fifty trillion cells; the cells are all autonomous, unique, and individuated, yet those cells are allured to each other, and they form a system. That system births life! A cancer cell is getting more sugar and then it is metastasizing, but it is not allured to the larger system, so it actually kills its host.

We are precisely at the place where the nature of the win/lose, game-theoretic metrics is now about to kill us.

We're faced with:

- Climate risk
- Nuclear risk
- Info/biotech risk, which creates multiple artificial intelligence applications

That's a disaster! What do we need to do?

We need to shift the system. **How do we shift the system? We shift the system by articulating a new vision.** The new vision is not a *complicated* system that breaks down but a system which is anti-fragile, as Nassim Taleb[37] says. Taleb does not quite get us there, and Snowden does not quite get *how the complex system works*.

A complex system is driven by intimacy and by a desire for intimacy because *it is* intimate, and *it is* driven by a desire for intimacy. Reality desires more intimacy. Evolution desires more intimacy. The trajectory of evolution is *allurement to more intimacy.*

What we are saying is that Conscious Evolution means to move from a complicated to a complex system. A complex system is a self-organizing system—the Universe, like a human body, like a slime mold—where *we have the intimacy of shared identity in the context of otherness.*

---

37 Nassim Nicholas Taleb introduced the concept of "antifragility" in his book *Antifragile: Things That Gain from Disorder.*

Shared identity means we're allured to each other, we are part of the same Reality, the same way that I am allured when I am hungry. My identity is with myself. I am hungry. I am allured to feed myself. That is level one.

Now, let's say I love you, and I love my family, and my kids, and my friends, and my close friends. I am allured to fill the needs of my family. I look at my family and I say, *Wow! Your need is my allurement.* That is huge!

Your need is my allurement. That is the beginning of a complex system!

Not just *my* need is my allurement, but *your* need is my allurement. That is the first level, that is egocentric intimacy. *Your need is my allurement* applies to me and my immediate circle.

WIDENING CIRCLES OF INTIMACY

What if I can be allured to my whole tribe?

When I move from egocentric intimacy to ethnocentric intimacy I can say to my whole tribe, *Your need is my allurement.* That's huge! Everybody in the tribe says: *your need is my allurement.* That's called nationalism. That's called patriotism! That's: *I am willing to die for my country.*

Now allurement needs to be clarified:

- We can have false allurement.
- We can have false nationalism.
- We can have false patriotism.
- We can have xenophobia.

But the deeper space is when we are—like in Evolutionary Church—all allured to each other. We look at each other in Evolutionary Church, and I say, *your need is my allurement* at the level of tribe, of the community. I don't just say it to my immediate survival people, not just to my wife and my son and my daughter, but I expand. I say to my whole tribe: *Your need is my allurement.*

And then imagine, my friends, we are the world! Remember the song *We Are the World?* Imagine if I move from egocentric intimacy to ethnocentric intimacy—and then I jump and I move to worldcentric intimacy.

At the level of worldcentric intimacy, if there is one human being on the planet that does not experience allurement, then there is one human being on the planet that does not experience the enchantment of their unique attraction. If there is one human being in the world that is hungry, this need allures me!

I experience *Your need is my allurement* at a worldcentric level. Literally, we are the world!

But then imagine that I wake up to the fourth level.

I wake up and I realize the truth of Reality. I realize that evolution is not a process *out there*. I realize that *I am part of the evolutionary context.*

- ◆ I live with an evolutionary relationship to life.
- ◆ I am living in an evolutionary context.
- ◆ I realize that evolution, the Universe, is awakening in me.

All of my allurement suddenly moves from worldcentric intimacy to cosmocentric intimacy.

All of a sudden, I am not satisfied to box cows in a little, small place where they can barely breathe just so that I can get a good piece of steak that makes me feel good for about 10 seconds, and I make a cow feel completely tortured for four months in order to accomplish that. And that cow, for the amount of meat that we eat, uses up enormous amounts of free-range, which is unbelievably important, and creates cascading negative effects in the biosphere.

Actually, no, no! I am not just allured to a piece of lamb chop, but I *feel* the larger context. I *can feel* the larger reality. I have cosmocentric intimacy. All of a sudden, *Your need is my allurement* applies:

- Not just to myself, to me and my immediate family—egocentric
- Not just to my "tribe" as in patriotism and nationalism—ethnocentric
- Not just to every human being—worldcentric

Your need is my allurement is a realization of cosmocentric intimacy. *I have cosmocentric intimacy!* Write that down and feel it! It is about claiming that! This is my intimacy, my allurement. That is huge! That changes the world. There's no one and no thing outside my circle of compassion.

Putting it another way would be to write: *My allurement is cosmocentric.* Ha! That is sexy! That is beautiful! That is alluring!

My allurement is cosmocentric. Oh my God!

ABOUT THE AUTHORS

Dr. Marc Gafni is a visionary world philosopher and futurist, one of the leading formulators of world spirituality and religion of our time, and a beloved teacher and public intellectual. He holds his doctorate in philosophy from Oxford University, as well as Orthodox rabbinic ordination. He co-founded the activist think tank, now called the Center for World Philosophy and Religion where he serves as the co-president with Dr. Zachary Stein. He also served with Barbara Marx Hubbard as co-president of the Foundation for Conscious Evolution, which he consented to lead at Barbara's request after her passing.

He is known for his "source code teachings"—including Unique Self theory and the Five Selves, the Amorous Cosmos, a Politics of Evolutionary Love, a Return to Eros, and Digital Intimacy—and has more than twenty books to his name, including the award-winning *Your Unique Self, A Return to Eros*, and three volumes of *Radical Kabbalah*.

He teaches on the cutting edge of philosophy in the West, helping to evolve a new d*harma* or meta-theory of Integral meaning that is helping to re-shape key pivoting points in global consciousness and culture, with the aim of participating in the articulation of what Dr. Gafni together with Dr. Stein and colleagues are calling CosmoErotic Humanism.

At the core of CosmoErotic Humanism is what Dr. Gafni and Dr. Stein are calling First Principles and First Values, Anthro-Ontology, and a Universal Grammar of Value. This is the ground of a new shared Universe story and a new narrative of identity for the new human and the new humanity. This is what they are calling the emergence from Homo sapiens to Homo amor.

This shared story rooted in First Principles and First Values can then serve as the matrix for a global ethos for a global civilization.

Together with Dr. Stein and Ken Wilber, Gafni is writing a series of seminal books under the collective pseudonym of David J. Temple, which intend to evolve the source code of consciousness and culture in response to the meta-crisis. The first of those books is *First Principles and First Values: Forty-Two Propositions on CosmoErotic Humanism, the Meta-Crisis, and the World to Come.*

Barbara Marx Hubbard (born Barbara Marx; December 22, 1929–April 10, 2019) was an American futurist, author, and public speaker. She is credited with the Wheel of Co-Creation and together with Dr. Gafni, the Wheel of Co-Creation 2.0, as well as the concepts of the Synergy Engine and the "birthing" of humanity.

As co-founder and president of the Foundation for Conscious Evolution and the chair, for the last five years of her life, of the Center for World Philosophy and Religion, she posited that humanity was on the threshold of a quantum leap if newly emergent scientific, social, and spiritual capacities were integrated to address global crises.

She was the author of seven books on social and planetary evolution. In conjunction with the Shift Network, she co-produced the worldwide "Birth 2012" multimedia event. She was also the subject of a biography by author Neale Donald Walsch, *The Mother of Invention: The Legacy of Barbara Marx Hubbard.* Deepak Chopra called her "the voice for conscious evolution."

In 1984, she was symbolically nominated for the vice presidency of the United States. She also co-chaired a number of Soviet-American Citizen Summits, introducing a new concept called SYNCON, to foster synergistic convergence with opposing groups. In addition, she co-founded the World Future Society and the Association for Global New Thought.

APPENDIX: SONGS

THE BATTLE HYMN OF THE REPUBLIC—JULIA WARD HOWE[1]

Mine eyes have seen the glory of the coming
  of the Lord.

He has trampled down the vintage
  where the grapes of wrath are stored.

He has loosed the fateful lightning
  of his terrible swift sword.

His truth is marching on.

HOW COULD ANYONE—LIBBY RODERICK [2]

How could anyone ever tell you
  you were anything less than beautiful?

How could anyone ever tell you
  you were less than whole?

How could anyone fail to notice
  that your loving is a miracle—
  how deeply you're connected to my soul?

---

1 Julia Ward Howe, The Battle Hymn of the Republic, 1862.
2 Libby Roderick, "How Could Anyone," on *If You See a Dream* (Turtle Island Records, 1990), CD.

I WANNA KNOW WHAT LOVE IS—FOREIGNER[3]

I've gotta take a little time,
a little time to think things over.
I better read between the lines,
in case I need it when I'm older.
(Whoa, ooh-ooh, ooh-ooh)

And this mountain, I must climb
feels like the world upon my shoulders,
and through the clouds, I see love shine,
it keeps me warm as life grows colder.

[Pre-Chorus]
In my life, there's been heartache and pain.
I don't know if I can face it again.
Can't stop now, I've travelled so far
to change this lonely life.

[Chorus]
I wanna know what love is.
I want you to show me.
I wanna feel what love is.
I know you can show me.
Oh, oh-oh, oh (ooh)

I'm gonna take a little time,
a little time to look around me.
I've got nowhere left to hide,
it looks like love has finally found me.

[Pre-Chorus]

[Chorus]

[Outro]

(And I wanna feel) I wanna feel what love is

---

3   Foreigner, "I Wanna Know What Love Is," recorded November 1984, on *Agent Provocateur*, Atlantic Records, vinyl LP.

(And I know) I know you can show me.
Let's talk about love.
(I wanna know what love is) The love that you feel inside.
(I want you to show me) And I'm feelin' so much love.
(I wanna feel what love is) No, you just cannot hide.
(I know you can show me) Yeah.
I wanna know what love is (Let's talk about love).
I want you to show me, I wanna feel.
(I wanna feel what love is) And I know, and I know.
I know you can show me (Yeah).
(I wanna know what love is) (I wanna know)
(I want you to show me) I wanna know, I wanna know, wanna know.
(I wanna feel what love is) (I wanna feel)
(I know you can show me).

HALLELUJAH—LEONARD COHEN[4]

Now, I've heard there was a secret chord
that David played, and it pleased the Lord.
But you don't really care for music, do you?
It goes like this, the fourth, the fifth,
the minor fall, the major lift.
The baffled king composing Hallelujah.

[Chorus]

Hallelujah, Hallelujah,
Hallelujah, Hallelujah.

Your faith was strong, but you needed proof.
You saw her bathing on the roof.
Her beauty and the moonlight overthrew you.
She tied you to a kitchen chair,
she broke your throne, and she cut your hair,
and from your lips she drew the Hallelujah.

---

4 Leonard Cohen, "Hallelujah", Various Positions, Columbia Records, 1984, LP.

[Chorus]

You say I took the name in vain,
I don't even know the name,
but if I did, well, really, what's it to you?
There's a blaze of light in every word,
it doesn't matter which you heard,
the holy or the broken Hallelujah.

[Chorus]

I did my best, it wasn't much.
I couldn't feel, so I tried to touch.
I've told the truth, I didn't come to fool you.
And even though it all went wrong,
I'll stand before the Lord of Song
With nothing on my tongue but Hallelujah.

OM NAMAH SHIVAAYA

Om Namah Shivaaya
Shivaaya namaha,
Shivaaya namah om
Shivaaya namaha, namaha Shivaaya
Shambhu Shankara namah Shivaaya,
Girijaa Shankara namah Shivaaya
Arunaachala Shiva namah Shivaaya

*I bow to the soul of all. I bow to my Self. I don't know who I am,
so I bow to you, Shiva, my own true Self. I bow to my teachers
who loved me with love. Who took care of me when I couldn't
take care of myself. I owe everything to them. How can I repay
them? They have everything in the world. Only my love is mine
to give, but in giving I find that it is their love flowing through
me back to the world…I have nothing. I have everything. I want
nothing. Only let it flow to you, my love… sing!*

INDEX

VOLUME 12 — Playing a Larger Game

LIST OF EPISODES